Don José
The Last Patrón

DON, JOSÉ

The Last Patrón

By José Ortiz y Pino III

Sunstone

Santa Fe, New Mexico

FIRST EDITION

Book Design: Sunstone
            Mina Yamashita, Art Director
Printed in the United States of America

Library of Congress Cataloging in Publication Data:

Ortiz y Pino, José, 1932–
     Don José, the last patrón.

     1. Ortiz y Pino, José. 2. Ortiz family.
3. Mexican Americans—New Mexico—Social conditions.
4. Mexican Americans—New Mexico—Biography.   I. Title.
F805.M5O776   978,9′0046872   81–8817
                                            AACR2
ISBN 0-86534-006-4 hard cover limited edition
ISBN 0-86534-007-2 soft cover edition

Published in 1981 by The Sunstone Press
            Post Office Box 2321
            Santa Fe, New Mexico 87501

To the stars who have witnessed,
and to the gnarled Tamarisk tree
which has sheltered History.
To my family, who encouraged me.

acknowledgements

I am grateful to my sister, Maria O. Catanach for her faith and for her numerous contributions which allowed this book to become a reality.

I extend my thanks and appreciation to Marion Steele who assisted me with the initial editing of the manuscript. His patience and help made the task a pleasant one.

Some of the photographs which appear in this book are courtesy of the State of New Mexico.

foreword

My father, Frank Ortiz y Davis, who left us seven years ago for a well-deserved eternal rest, is here with me as I review a hundred years – 1852-1952 – of my family's colorful history. It is not only my family's history, but more importantly, the history of a people – a proud and dedicated people who witnessed and lived under the Patrón system. This was a system or manner of living that today's historians either fail to represent correctly or else completely ignore.

I lived a part of this Patrón system during my early life and had the great experience of having witnessed it from both sides. Today, when I observe how many of our Hispanic generation have too little understanding of their history, I hope this book will serve to remind them that in the time of their forefathers, respect for authority and loyalty to those whom they served signified the size of a man.

The Patrón system prevailed in New Mexico at that time because it was right for the times. The Patrón or benefactor, provided a livelihood and security for his people, and in turn, the people provided him with work and loyalty. In some cases the Patrón system was abused and people were forced to live in an enslaved condition. This story of Don José Ortiz y Pino is the life of a patrón who did not enslave his people, but rather gave them love and dignity. With the help of these people, he created an empire which survived into the 1950s.

Don José was a man of his time. A unique man, embodying great strength and gentleness. The picture of him on the cover of this book speaks of this to us.

Following the Afterword is a descriptive listing of one hundred of the native medicinal herbs which have played an important part in the lives of my people. Their uses and the cures which they bring I feel will be of help to the readers in understanding more about the wonderful world of herbs.

It is with an humble feeling I bring to you a dream that was, that still is, and will remain with mankind until history down the road calls once again for *The Last Patrón*.

José Ortiz y Pino III
Fall 1980

Bird's eye view of Galisteo.

Don José
The Last Patrón

map of galisteo

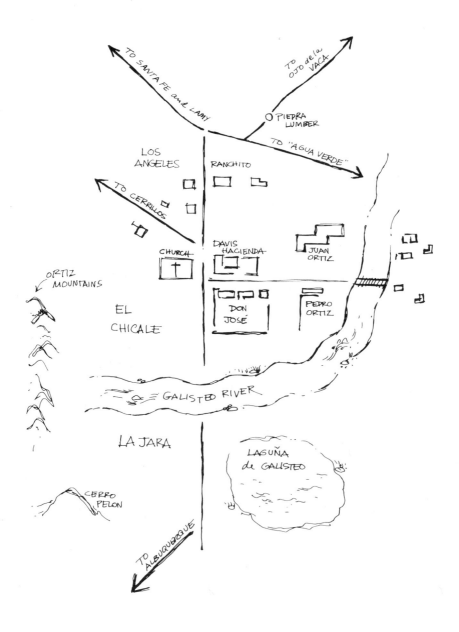

one

Galisteo!

The solitude and peace that prevails in this serenely magnificent basin holds a magical effect on all those who ever crossed it on their way to Santa Fe. The sound and smell of History permeates the rolling hills and low lying mesas. All around, there is evidence of the early settlers. One senses their spirit of sacrifice and the great challenges they met. They had much to be proud of for they had to unravel the mystery of this strange, haunting land. Time has marched on since the first settlers came here, but the land has only become more entrancing and Galisteo lives on.

We pick up this story about twenty years after the great Civil War. The War had touched the village of Galisteo only briefly.

Don Juan Ortiz, my great-grandfather, was lighting his cigar after a big meal of carne asada and his favorite, pan del orno (bread baked in the outdoor oven). His two favorite sons were sitting at his feet in front of the huge, mud fireplace, partly looking at the wood crackling and sparking, and also trying to listen to their father's tales of his life as a trader, hauling freight from Durango, Mexico in the past, and in the present, making the long hauls from St. Louis and Kansas City to Santa Fe and Galisteo. All his hauling was done by wagons pulled by mighty oxen. One hundred wagons and five hundred oxen – what a sight that must have been! Only the people of the times could appreciate what he endured. Don Juan told the sleepy boys about the storms, the Indians and Outlaws, and the other adversities that only he, the early freight-hauler, realized and understood. Juan Ortiz was not large in stature, but a giant in courage. As he sat there talking to his sons, José and Pedro, his wife, Concepción, was in the comedor with the other sons – Herman, Facundo and Onofré, and the two daughters, Margarita and Trinidad. Here was the continuation of a famous family tree, for Concepción was the daughter of Juana Rascon and Nicholas de Jesús Pino. Nicholas Pino's grandfather was Pedro Bautista Pino, born in Tomé, 1750, the only delegate from the Spanish Colony in New Mexico to help draw up the first Spanish Constitution in Cádiz, Spain in 1814. Juana Rascón was also the niece of the first Vicar General to the Province. So with this kind of recent history in their background, you could feel that this family had been marked by destiny to continue providing service and would contribute greatly to the history of this New Mexico.

Juan asked Pedro to add some more wood to the fire and continued to visit with his sons. He asked, "José! Pedro! What would you, if God wills, do with your lives?"

Pedro answered promptly and directly, "Papa Juan, I want to own vast herds of sheep and maybe even have a big store and freight business like you."

"Good, my son! And you, José?"

José glanced into the fire and saw so much there, but he did not say it all, except, "Papa Juan, I want to be the largest land-owner in the Territory, and I want to help people."

"Good, José!" Juan answered, and a smile came to his tired face. The other boys would choose someday. And the girls. Well! – in the old families they had only one goal, to love their husbands and raise fine children.

Concepción walked into the great sala and softly told the boys that it was time to retire. As they left the room, Concepción walked over to Juan and, always the devoted wife and mother, kissed her Juan and asked, "What were you talking about?"

Juan smiled and answered, "The future of our family and our people. God has been good to us and we must never quit thanking Him. Now to bed for tomorrow will soon be here." Galisteo was soon asleep.

But what about Galisteo, located in Northern New Mexico, about twenty-one miles south of Santa Fe, on the Galisteo Creek? Here it was founded in the middle of five famous Indian pueblos: San Cristóbal, Chee, San Lazaro, San Marcos and Pueblo Galisteo. The Spaniards had first seen this area in 1591 when Castano de Sosa passed through on his expedition. He named the area San Lucas. Oñate, the first colonizer of New Mexico, called it Santa Ana. And they went on changing its name until the present Galisteo. It was the Galisteo Indians who helped take over Santa Fe during the Rebellion of 1680, and so once again Galisteo jumped on the bandwagon of historical events.

Pueblo Galisteo, which lies north of the Spanish settlement about three-quarters of a mile, housed the Tewa Indians, and the Pueblo was called Tanoque. Many famous missionaries worked amongst these Indians. Friar Juan Bernal is the most important, as he was in charge of the small mission during the Rebellion of 1680. He was killed inside the mission on the day of the uprising, and all the natives were ordered to burn their rosaries, crucifixes, and holy articles, and the mission was desecrated. Many of the Spanish settlers living in the Spanish village of Galisteo were murdered, among them, relatives of Don Juan Ortiz. The proud Spanish settlers returned after the reconquest, and by the early 1700s, the Spaniards were in complete control.

The family of Juan Ortiz and many other settlers began their task of creating a new Spain.

Don Juan awakened to a beautiful day. After a warm and hearty breakfast of *chili colorado* with *chaquehue*, a blue corn meal mush, and delicate flour tortillas, Don Juan walked over to the side of his hacienda which housed his office and store. There would be people waiting – sheepherders, vaqueros, freight drivers and villagers.

"Buenos días! Le de Dios, Don Juan!"

Don Juan answered, "Y a Usted también, Camilo!" Camilo was his store clerk and had been with Don Juan since he was a child – Don Juan had raised many children besides his and Concepción's. As they entered the long, hall-type room to light the morning fire, you could see long rows, shelf upon shelf of staple goods, materials, rope, saddles and the many items that the small village needed to continue its daily living.

José and Pedro as well as the other children would visit their father and continually be amazed by all the wonderful things that made up the village's only store. The smell of drying herbs and the barrels of beautiful candies together with new hardware and pungent harness created an unbelievable scent.

Herders were assigned their daily duties, and vaqueros were dispatched on their routes for the day. The whole country was open. Fences were unheard of. Everyone who had been waiting for Don Juan was respectfully attended to. By midday one could find Don Juan sitting in his favorite straw chair covered with a deer hide, peacefully smoking a cigar. He was tired and satisfied. He would tell himself in these moments of peace that soon he must leave, and he prayed that his children would be ready to carry on. It had taken years of hard work in a land that had been good to him to build up his business and his claims to some fine lands.

There were other families in the town who also had worked hard and were seeing the fruits of their efforts. Amongst them was the Pino family who was closely related to the Ortiz. There were, too, the Chavez, Sandoval, Leyba, Gonzales, Luna and many other families who at this time and period, 1880, gave the village a population of some eight hundred people.

So many things did Don Juan think of, and as he reflected on God's gifts, an endless stream of people walked into the store. But Camilo would not bother Don Juan, as the clerk efficiently dispatched the clients. Don Juan thought about his children's education, which ones would try to be good students and which ones would soon lose interest. He wondered and prayed for Concepción, his wife, for she also would have to be strong and patient when it was time for him to leave. "So many unfinished jobs," he thought. "But I have tried to do them all well." The dreams that his children had, especialy José and Pedro, he would love to see them fulfilled for he felt that truly these two sons would establish their own history. The many workers and servants who had so loyally placed their hands in his for so many years...Yes!, he would reward them and Yes!, God had already given him his reward.

Old Galisteo church at top of the hill, built in 1614.

two

José and his family worked hard and always Don Juan's eye was on them. The herds of sheep started to grow and the store and freight business continued to prosper. A few pieces of land that Don Juan had given José were planted in corn and grains. Galisteo and its people were blessed by plentiful moisture, winter and summer.

One day as José rode past the Josefa Ortiz home, he caught a glance of Pablita, whom he always considered a baby. Now no longer a child, she smiled at him. Here truly was a fine woman! "Why have I waited so long to see this girl as a woman?" he thought. Daily almost he had seen her, but now he was seeing her for the first time. His heart was hers. "But only time will give us her answer." Pablita had always admired this tall man, and she felt his power that day.

José was not yet called "Don". This would take time and respect by his peers and workers. As he kept a distant eye on Pablita, his main attention was focused on his business of increasing his holdings. José needed a place to operate from, for his father's place was too small for all the animals and functions that he dreamed of. Don Juan had given him a nice parcel in the center of the village, with the Galisteo River running through it. On the east side, his brother Pedro was busy restoring Nicholas Pino's old home and also preparing for the future. José would walk this land of his in the evenings or early mornings thinking, "I'll place a corral here, a building there, and over there the great house I'll build for Pablita. Oh, how I'd like to speak with her!" But customs were strong and traditions even stronger. He must wait until all the proper and traditional events could take place: proper introductions, visitations by his father and mother to her family, notes of acceptance of visiting privileges, and on and on. It seemed an endless way to say, "Pablita, I just want to talk with you. Pablita, if you could only see what plans I have for us. I want our house just the way you want it, for we will have many children. The girls will be beautiful like you, and the boys strong like me!"

José was a big man now, in size six feet and over, with beautiful features and a strong moustache that made his tone of voice seem even stronger than it was – it seemed to become very authoritative when he felt it was necessary.

It was time for José to start his own hacienda, and the beautiful plot of land in the middle of the village would become his headquarters. Men were hired to start building corrals and barns, fencing and cross fencing. Handsome stables were built along with two or three work sheds. Trees were planted – apples, peaches, cherries and above all his favorite, pears. His men worked hard for him. When they ran out of things to do on the crop lands or the caring for the sheep and a few cattle, all extra work was devoted to the hacienda.

"But something is missing, I feel." The answer was in front of him as he looked at his headquarters going up. "I must have an office. And why not a store? I'll not be competing with my father, as he already is winding down his operation." Which was true. Don Juan was tired and when José mentioned his idea of his own store, Don Juan said, "Fine, José! I will be your best customer."

And so with hard work and patience a building was started, facing the main village street. Adobe by adobe, soon a large hall-shaped building started to take form. José was proud. "And there next to it, facing the same street will be Pablita's and my home!"

Late October, cattle and sheep must be sorted. Some will be kept, others sold, and the fattest will be slaughtered to furnish meat during the long, cold winter. So many preparations to greet the winter! José sometimes wondered about this great master plan that society labelled "seasons". He realized that only God could explain it, for the seasons served a definite purpose. Spring, he knew, brought promise and life; summer created growth and progress; fall was the time to reap the harvest of spring and summer; then winter, a time for all – plants, beasts and man – to rest, a time to plan, and of course, to keep warm.

He felt cold this late October morning as he looked across the street from his still unfinished store. Across the street at an angle was Pablita's home, a truly beautiful home with the most magnificent courtyard. Yes! He had heard the many stories of the Ortiz hacienda, how it had served as protection against attacking Indians, how later it had housed Union and Confederate troops and other interesting people for whom Pablita's mother had provided shelter. Just then, Pablita came into view in front of the hacienda. She was accompanied by Jade, a black girl whom her mother, Doña Josefita, had raised. Jade and her sister Ivy had been thrown from a train at Kennedy Crossing, a mile and a half west of Galisteo. The two little black girls had been raised and loved by Doña Josefita, and Jade became Pablita's constant shadow.

José called out to Pablita, "Buenos días, Pablita!"

Back came her cheerful answer, "Buenos días, José!"

José walked across the street toward her. Jade tugged at Pablita's dress and said, "Come on! Come on! You must not talk with him here in the street!" But Pablita held her ground as the large figure of José loomed over them.

"With your permission, Pablita, I would like to come and call on you and your family one of these days," he said.

Pablita smiled as Jade frowned, and answered, "Please do, José!" She then excused herself and disappeared around the corner of the hacienda. José felt even taller and his deep, powerful eyes at that moment could have competed with the morning star.

Pablita hurried into the house with her shadow and found her mother, Josefita, discussing the day's chores with her father, Sylvester Davis. Pablita would wait and tell her mother alone, for she knew that her father would receive the news from Josefita. A great deal of respect was held for the head of the family. This family was a little different as there were actually two heads! Josefita was a very strong willed and determined woman. Since early age, she had been competitive with men. She could ride, rope, saddle and work with horses as well as, and sometimes better than most men. Her father, Juan Ortiz Grande, and her mother, Pablita, always felt that Josefita needed a strong man to handle her. They had nine children, and Josefita was outstanding.

Outstanding, that is, until she met the quiet, handsome 'gringo' from Kentucky. Sylvester Davis had headed west after the Civil War. He had served in the Confederate Army; many claimed he had been a Captain in the Rebel Army, but he never spoke much about it, or his former life in the South. Sylvester came in from the northeast part of New Mexico and an interesting journal tells of his life and time there. He came into Galisteo one cold winter day and, looking for a place to rest and keep warm, was directed by some villagers to Josefa's hacienda. From the moment that these two people saw each other, one could tell a new chapter would start in their lives. The whole village would be affected. Such were the opposite strengths of Josefita and Sylvester. They would marry and have twelve children, Pablita being one of the oldest.

Pablita finally caught her mother alone and told her what José had asked that morning. Josefita was elated and said, "It is fine! He is very handsome and all the women of the village, married and unmarried, speak of him and his powerful presence. I will speak to your father, and we will await his visit. Now, Jade, don't you be telling everyone you see! We don't want to sound too excited."

"No, Doña Josefita, I won't. I never will," the girl replied. Jade loved to talk and sometimes it was impossible to stop her – it usually took a good pinch to do the trick!

Pablita was so excited that for that day and until José showed up four days later, her feet never touched the ground.

José was excited when he saw his father, Don Juan. José explained his feelings and intentions for Pablita. Don Juan promised to get personal approval from Sylvester in the next day or so. That way José's visit would comply with custom.

Everything had been arranged when José knocked at the large wooden door of the Davis hacienda. Sylvester greeted him and asked him to be seated in front of a large, roaring fire burning in a very odd-shaped fireplace. "It's almost bell-shaped. But, so crooked!" José thought. As he and Sylvester conversed about José's progress on the new store and his other business enterprises, José felt very comfortable. Presently, Doña Josefita entered the sala and after greeting José warmly, offered to bring them a cup of tea.

"What would you like, José? Manzanilla, yerba buena or perhaps some mestela (an herbal tea made with oshá root and whiskey)?" José asked for the mestela, for he felt he could use it.

A beautiful and warm sight to José came through the door with the refreshments. It was Pablita. "Hello, José! It was nice of you to come." she said. José stood and smiled broadly as he returned her greeting.

"Thank you, Pablita. Won't you join us?" the father asked, and the conversation went from subject to subject. The visit was soon over, much to José's and Pablita's dismay. Much had been said by Pablita and José, of course, with their eyes and smiles. Sylvester led José to the door and bade him farewell, but of course asking José to come visit again soon.

After their guest had departed, Sylvester, Josefita and Pablita talked awhile, and from the kind, receptive things her father and mother said, Pablita knew they liked José. She also knew that after José made a few more visits, his father and mother would be over to ask for her hand in marriage to José.

Winter moved on and the villagers kept busy with the winter lifestyle: wood hauling, feeding livestock and work that could be done indoors, such as mending harness. José's construction stopped during the very cold weather, but whenever a nice day appeared, a little work was always done. His mind worked during cold winter nights as he planned the course of his life and now also his life with the beautiful Pablita. He was never too tired though to sit in front of the fireplace with the village *viejitos* (old men) to listen to them trying to outdo each other with tales of witches and devils and folklore and just plain lies, told with class. José enjoyed their stories and learned from their wisdom. He learned from them as he listened.

One cold night, Señor Celestino came by and recounted one of the most fascinating *cuentos* (folk stories) he had ever heard. Celestino pulled his chair close to the fire, taking a long pull at his pipe, and began.

"In a small village nestled in the mountains of northern New Mexico, an agricultural village where vast herds of sheep, goats and cattle were grazed, many men and women were employed in that particular business. In this small village there was one family that was one of the hardest working – the Tenorio family. Old Jesús Tenorio was the head of the family. He and his wife, Feliciana, had six children, five sons and one beautiful daughter who came late in life. Her name was Suzanna. She was about fourteen years old when this story unravels. She was considered by everyone in the village to be such a fine young lady.

"All of a sudden, Suzanna took on some kind of illness, an illness that didn't seem to be involved in any way physically. She became quiet and strange. The neighbors and her relatives, her aunts, uncles and brothers in particular, noticed a change taking place in this girl who enjoyed baking bread and taking off her shoes and walking down the river, running across fields carrying lunch and little pieces of tortillas to her father as he tended the herds. Here was a girl who had lost all of her enthusiasm. The villagers wondered why Suzanna no longer had the will to live. The villagers told the parents that perhaps they should consult one of the *brujos* or consult one of the *curanderos* from some other village. Up to this time there were no *curanderos* in this village; the closest one was about thirty miles away.

"Now the *curandero*, the person who dealt with herbal medicine, was finally sought and brought to check Suzanna. He prescribed various medications in the form of teas and poltices for application. She was to use these for a number of days to see if there was any change or reaction. But Suzanna made no endeavors to get well in any way. The Tenorio family threw up its hands in vain. Finally they were told by other friends, "Well, well! Get the *brujo*. He will surely, surely find the solution if this young lady is perhaps possessed by the devil or there is a bad spiritual aura around her. Somebody might have given her the evil eye."

"In this village, as in other northern New Mexico villages, when you *hizo ojo*, this was a bad omen. When someone made the evil eye, it could change your entire life and could kill you. So the Tenorio family hesitantly – because they were fine Catholics – called on the *brujo*.

"The *brujo* in the area was known as Juanito. He was a small man, a sheepherder, and the lonely type of a man who would spend many, many months with his herds up in the mountains and come down only whenever he felt that he needed to look over his friends or when his friends or others would call on him for the powers he possessed. Then he would make a special trip. When he was summoned by the Tenorio family, Juanito came from the hills. Upon entering their house, he stood like a statue; he was very bewildered; he could not move. The members of the Tenorio family also stood in awe, observing him. He seemed to be possessed, and at that instant, his face started to change color. As it did, Suzanna ran out the door as fast as she possibly could. The family observed, as they hollered at her to come back, a black object chasing her. The brujo unfroze at that instant. He sat down and told the family he would work to do his best but that he would have to find Suzanna.

"The day went by and the search took place. There was no trace of Suzanna. Late in the evening as some of the herders were coming into the village with their herds for the night, they came upon the body of Suzanna lying in one of the open meadows. "No more breath! She has gone to rest." The village went into mourning. The beautiful young lady was brought to her parents. The bells started to give their death toll, informing the village that one of them had gone to meet her Maker. The plans were set for the *velorio* (the wake) and for the *entierro* (the burial). Now, in this village, there was a large hall used by the people from all over the region for their *velorios*. The Tenorio family, having many friends and relatives, were fortunate the hall was available to them for the evening of the *velorio*. Many people would travel long distances to pay their condolances to the family, and always food was served to them.

"The wake was held the following evening and the hall was filled with people. Suzanna lay in state amidst sprays of flowers picked from gardens and bouquets of wild flowers and sages gathered by her friends to adorn her casket. Viewing the beautiful Suzanna, her family and friends could not find it in their hearts to believe that the Great Creator could so quickly and so ungratefully take such a fine young woman away in the prime of her youth.

"The padre came from a distance to say a rosary for Suzanna. As the rosary was taking place in the long hall, the bells tolled very gently across the street in the old mission. The people were getting along with the rosary and final mysteries when a great wind, a great noise was heard at the entrance. The two huge wooden doors which were at the entrance to this old hall were flung open. The scene became subdued chaos. The people were transfixed as two huge, black creatures – animal-like, dog-like – with flaming eyes, ran through the center of the assembled people and snatched Suzanna out of the coffin. They ran just as fast out the doors with the body. It took but a moment, but it seemed years before the people responded...confusion, absolute confusion and fear in their hearts! Juanito, the *brujo*, stood before the crowd and said, 'No one must follow 'til morning...'til the first rays of the sun shine on this valley. Everyone must wait here. No one must follow. The horses can be arranged for and brought out and saddled, but no one must move 'til morning.'

"The people responded quietly and went to their homes. The men assembled their mounts and prepared themselves for the first rays of sun. As it peeked in from the east, they set out in search of Suzanna. There were thirty or forty men of the village, accompanied by Juanito.

"As they left the village, they saw a great column of smoke rising to the south. They hurried their mounts and upon approaching the smoke, they saw a clump of cactus burning intensely. As they drew near, they saw the body of Suzanna on this clump of cactus and another object lying at her feet. The fire seemed to extinguish itself and the body of Suzanna was not in any way burned. The men stared at the grotesque sight. There was the body of a man lying at the bottom of the cactus. The body was torn into shreds, almost like animals had had a tug of war with it. On closer identification, they made it out to be Suzanna's uncle, Suzanna's mother's favorite brother.

"Juanito, the *brujo*, said, 'Take her back for burial. This must all end. And take what can be picked up of him back, for tomorrow we must continue with our lives.' With that Juanito disappeared.

"The people took Suzanna and her uncle to the village for burial. Days went by, and months, and still the mystery was never solved. Fear existed among the villagers and particularly amongst Suzanna's family. They did not understand the strange things that had happened without any explanation until many years later, when a young man who was a boy of eight at the time of Suzanna's death came forth, and in his boisterous way said that one time before Suzanna got sick, he had followed her when she was taking lunch to her uncle's home. He had heard screaming when Suzanna went in the door. He had peeked in the window and saw Suzanna's uncle ravishing her, mutilating her beautiful young body. Suzanna tore away from him and left the house screaming.

After that she went into her depression, for the greatest gift she had to give had been taken away from her by someone she had trusted and loved so much as her uncle.

"The story ends with her uncle paying for his deed. And the black dog of the village also paying for his deed. Among the villagers of northern New Mexico, black dogs represent both good and bad luck."

Everyone in the room was absolutely quiet, no sound had been made as Señor Celestino recounted his bit of folklore. His was an incredible story, but of course this land was also incredible and mysterious.

José told his father, "That *cuento* was hard to beat!"

"You haven't heard Doña Luisa's stories yet," Don Juan answered. "Wait until she comes over."

A date was set for Don Juan and Doña Concepción to call on the Davis family to ask for Pablita's hand in marriage to José. The then properly engaged couple decided to marry the coming June. Pablita was in for the most exciting period of her young life. As custom demanded – and the joining of these two prominent families called for – there would be a grand fiesta, the sort the village of Galisteo had never seen!

Spring came. It was calving and lambing time. José and his brother Pedro helped each other with their herds and every spare man was given a job to do. The Galisteo area was slowly but surely becoming a well-known livestock producing area. Many of the villagers were also raising sheep, cattle and horses. The lands around Galisteo were still free and mostly ownerless, with the exception of Federal lands. The community was thriving and during this period of 1896 over 700 people enjoyed the peace and prosperity of Galisteo. Cantinas and small stores were opening. Festive events were held at the drop of a hat.

José would complete his store and office by early spring, then he and Pablita would plan their home. He would visit Pablita but they were always chaperoned either by Jade or Ivy. Custom dictated the engaged couple be attended until *la luna de miel* (the honeymoon).

three

José's herds of sheep were increasing and he needed more land, so with every extra dollar he would make from now on, he began his plan of acquiring as much land as he could. The people of the village could sense José's ambition, but they could not understand his driving manner. Slowly they would learn to respect him and eventually call him Don José.

The wedding day arrived and all the months of exhausting preparations by the two families created and presented one of the most beautiful weddings and celebrations Galisteo had ever known. The wedding was held in the village church, which was adorned with flowers from the floor to the rafters. So many people were in attendance that only a tenth of them actually witnessed the ceremony inside the small church. The crowd spilled into the main street and backed out almost to the river bridge.

The bride came down the aisle in a magnificent creation shipped from Chihuahua, Mexico. It was a white satin and lace gown, resplendent with thousands of pearls. The jewelry she wore was from Spain, brought here by her forefathers.

The groom, of course, looked absolutely handsome and his height presented an overwhelming power on the guests.

After the ceremony the bride and groom were escorted to the Davis hacienda across the street. Waiting for the couple and their guests were ten of the best steers from Doña Josefita's and Sylvester's herd which had been barbequed for two days over a well-tended piñon fire. Tables were laid throughout the courtyard and the adjoining orchard. Gallons of beans, red chili, green chili and posole were set at strategic points. There were huge baskets of tortillas and bread from the outdoor ovens piled on tables. Barrels of wine had been brought from Bernalillo and there were casks of homemade apple cider and, of course, white lightning or *mula*, as the locals called it. Everywhere you turned, musicians and solo guitarists blended in a mass musical tribute, creating a fiesta that would never be forgotten.

The festivities continued into the early morning hours with dancing and toasting that gave the more than one thousand guests a good excuse to forever compare this with other weddings.

After a brief honeymoon, José and his Pablita moved into José's father's house, where they would stay until their home was finished.

José worked very hard with his various business ventures, and his store would be ready. The corrals and other buildings were already in use and much activity was taking place daily at his hacienda – minus the house. When José found spare time, usually about mid-morning, he would go to the recently completed schoolhouse where he would help to teach small children a little bit of arithmetic and to read. José had been fortunate to have good tutoring early in life from traveling teachers who came by the village from time to time. José received a great deal of satisfaction in being able to help these children, whom he called *mis hijitos*, my children. In years to come, many people would hear the word *hijito* coming from his lips, for to José, people were more important than just plain people.

The home Pablita and José planned was finished and they moved in. They eagerly planned their own family. About the same time, Don Juan died. He had been ill for some time, but his death was a turning point in his sons' lives. José and Pedro, especially, would miss Don Juan like the plants miss the sun. The funeral was a typical Spanish spectacle, with its religious fervor.

As the bell of the village church, Our Lady of Remedies, tolled announcing the death of a villager, the town sent children, old men or someone to inquire, "For whom does the bell toll?"

"Don Juan Ortiz left quietly this early morning."

The village received the news with great sadness and loneliness for Don Juan was truly loved, first as a man, then as a respected Patrón – not an absolute Patrón, but a more subtle one for the times.

Preparations were made by all the villagers to accompany Don Juan and his family in their hour of sorrow. Children were sent into the fields to gather wild flowers and fragrant plants of all kinds. The women prepared large quantities of food: posole, menudo, beans, chili, stacks of tortillas, sweet rolls, biscochitos and gallons of coffee and tea. The families of the village would bring these foods on the first night of the *velorio* and every night thereafter until Don Juan was laid to rest.

A message was sent to the priest in Pecos who also served the Galisteo parish. The priest would try to arrive in a day or so to bury Don Juan. The patriarch was laid out in the great sala of his home, and all the flowers were placed around his simple, wooden coffin. In those days, the body was washed and dressed and the flowers around the coffin took care of the embalming process with their beautiful scent. A rosary was led by his good friend, Manuel Leyba. People filed in and paid their respects. This custom was called giving *el pésamo*. After the rosary, food was served to all those in attendance. Praying and visiting, including a little drinking, would last late into the night and early morning hours. After two more nights of the *velorio* came the day of burial.

The padre had arrived the night before and he stayed at Doña Josefita's Inn where a room was always kept for visiting padres. Josefita and Jade attended to the comforts of the visitors.

Church bells rang their sorrowful toll, as Don Juan's casket was carried into the church for the Funeral Mass. After the Mass, the coffin was carried in a fine wagon and drawn by Don Juan's horses. The procession wound its way to the small cemetery on a hill behind the church. There, a few more prayers were said, and Don Juan's family said their last farewells to Don Juan.

He was laid to rest among other members of the family.

Galisteo homes.

four

The era of Don Juan Ortiz had come to an end and the future belonged to his children. Don Juan's properties were dispersed according to his will. José received some fine parcels in the village proper as well as grazing lands to the north of Galisteo along the river. Pedro received lands to the west of Galisteo, as well as the old property of Pedro Bautista Pino. The other living children also received their share. Doña Concepción kept the family hacienda and all of Don Juan's personal effects. Servants were remembered with small gifts of money and land.

During this period, other people from outside the village began to become interested in acquiring lands, for at this time the Federal government began implementation of the first Homestead Act, which allowed a person or persons to settle on a one hundred sixty acre parcel of land. After a period of years, if they built a house on it and fenced it, they acquired a complete patent deed for the property. There were many variations to this law prior to 1910, but in effect, to comply with the law was very easy. You didn't have to build a large house – a one-room cabin was sufficient. The fencing could be started or partial You could get away with just living off-and-on the land occasionally. All you had to do was file and send the location of your land claim in, together with its township and section location.

It was now the beginning of a new century, and Galisteo, having known Spanish, Mexican and now American rule, was ready for its real place in history. Adventurers were arriving from the eastern United States and among them were many merchants and traders. With the Homestead Act, José knew it was time to move and move fast! Don Juan was gone. The title of patrón belonged to José and now he would be Don José, for his holdings and his position were fast becoming the mainstay of the village. He had in his employ most of the families who were not self-employed. Don José felt the land question would be the center of his quest.

His store was now in full operation, and here all the needed supplies of the village were available. It is important to describe the store for it would play an important part in the life and work of Don José.

Facing the main village street was a long ramp. The length of it greeted the visitor. Two huge doors opened on the ramp and as you walked in to your left was a long counter that served as the business and pay area. In front of this counter were bins and shelves of staples and every food item available in the territory. Beyond those bins and shelves were hardware and candies of all kinds. To your right as you entered, were clothing in cases, shoes by the dozens, all sorts of wearing apparel and a fine selection of materials and threads. A huge iron stove was in the center of the room and, at a distance, two chairs caught your eye. Opposite the two chairs was the door that led to Don José's office. Hanging on the ceiling of the store were all kinds of harness, rope and drying herbs, for Don José was a believer in the powerful world of herbs. An adjoining room to the east of the building held a mouse-and-rat proof enclosure where wheat, flour and meal were kept. Under this same room a small basement held potatoes, onions and other items which needed to be kept extra cool. The whole store was a magical place. Everywhere you looked you would see a different item, from pocket knives and pocket watches to rouge and lip salve for the ladies. But the two big chairs dominated the store.

In his office were a huge oak desk and a number of chairs and everywhere hanging from the ceiling and on the walls were a varied assortment of artifacts and guns. Sheepskins provided the carpeting. Indeed, there was no finer store and office in this area of the territory.

Don José called his storekeeper into his office. "Valentino, I'd like for you to have Señor Raul Sandoval come to see me if he comes to the store today."

"Yes, Patrón. Anything else?" Valentino asked.

"No. I'll visit with you later," Don José answered.

Raul Sandoval came in later that morning and Valentino ushered him over to the Patrón's office. "Here's Raul, Patrón!"

"Gracias!" Don José answered as he and Raul greeted each other. Soon both men were in deep conversation. Don José was proposing a venture which could make Raul some extra money as well as give him security. "Raul, I'd like you and your four older brothers to allow me to file papers on your behalf on a section of land that adjoins some of our Ortiz Land Grant that lies to the south of the village. Each of you can claim one hundred sixty acres and live on them. I will help you build a house and give you a few cows and sheep. After a number of years, I will give you a top price for your efforts and you will deed the land to me."

"Don José, this will help us all. Our money is little and what food we get, you are the one who gives it to us. A favor should be repaid with a favor," Raul said. "But how will we manage, just living there with a few animals on these lands?"

"I will buy your surplus animals, and also give you an open account here at my store. Don't worry about what you owe me until you deed the land to me and I pay you. Then we can deduct your bills you owe me. You may also stay on those lands while I am alive, for I will not leave you without shelter," Don José told him.

Raul was happy to comply and he knew of others who would appreciate such an arrangement with Don José.

The forefathers of Don José had been given a grant of land by the King of Spain in gratitude for their service to the Crown. The forefathers were allowed to pick a high rise on a special piece of country they wanted, and then as far as they could see in every direction was theirs. The Ortiz Land Grant was such a grant, not surveyed, and without marked boundaries. It was yours if you were man or woman enough to keep it! So the family would lay claim to all the Galisteo Basin, and what they wanted to hold on to, they would. The rest could go its way. Much land had been staked out and marked by the Ortiz family and passed on to their heirs. Don José would secure his claims with fencing and brute force, if necessary, but always ending large or complicated land problems by giving a little – and salvaging a lot.

The federal or territorial governments did not wish to recognize these Spanish Royal grants and Mexican government grants, and thus the Homestead Act served as a tool to help distribute large portions of these lands.

Statehood was rapidly coming to New Mexico, and when it arrived in 1912, Don José's and Pablita's family also arrived with it. In total, José and Pablita had eighteen children, but because of the high infant mortality rate, only five would survive into their twenties. One son survived. This son would be Don José's star, a special star whom he would dream of and wish for when he observed the celestial bodies in the early morning or late at night. The extra chair he placed in his office was to be for Francisco Ortiz y Davis. His son carried both his mother's maiden name and his father's. But Francisco would finally just be called "Frank" as the Anglo influence crept into the area.

Statehood brought with it many changes. The ones felt most by Don José and Galisteo were political. Politics started to play a strong part in the development of the State. There was great jockeying to gain power with this new tool. Don José recognized this new method and proceeded to join the power-brokers or king-makers. He chose the Republican Party, at least for this period. A handful of men in this part of the State controlled the political machine, and the men behind the machine were men with money and influence. This was the rank that Don José joined and his office became the scene of many important political decisions in the history of New Mexico.

Raul Sandoval brought his brothers to Don José. An agreement was struck and papers were filed with the Federal Land Office. After a few years, Don José would own another section of land. Many men joined the procession as Don José was gaining high respect as a man who would keep his promises. Don José concentrated on the lands to the south and west of Galisteo, the areas known as *el cerro pelón*. It was a large, bald mesa the Indians used to call the sun dial. As he acquired it, he stocked this country with more sheep. People who were not homesteading for him were soon joining his fast growing army of sheepherders, campers and vaqueros. The pay was fair for the times, but even better was the open line of credit Don José extended at his store.

As he noticed his hard working men patronizing cantinas that had been started in the village, Don José again felt something was missing. "I must provide my men with all their needs!" he said. So he built a new building to the east of the store. It was called *La Cantinita*.

The headquarters area of Don José cointinued to grow, and soon almost a town within a town covered the beautiful acres which Don José had prepared so diligently to serve as his center of operations.

Don José would try to work in his office every morning, setting his plans and giving them direction. The days were filled with innumerable interruptions, but youth and its vigor were on Don José's side. More than that, he felt a total dedication. Without faith in his Creator, he would have faltered. Don José believed and lived a life of positive thinking. In order to allow the emotional and mental aspect of his life to be free and uncluttered, he felt a healthy body was essential. Upon awakening every morning, be it at three o'clock or a little later, Don José would drink two or three glasses of water from the hand-dug well outside his and Pablita's bedroom door, and then he would prepare for the day by wielding a fifteen pound sledge hammer and pounding a huge log that had been buried in the ground by his men for this purpose. The log, maybe thirty-six inches in diameter and four feet long, was buried close to his office door. In his lifetime, hundreds of these logs were shattered to pieces by Don José's pounding with the sledge. This exercise lasted about fifteen minutes. He firmly believed if a healthy mind created a healthy body, a healthy body created a healthy mind. Then he would take a walk and inspect every inch of his headquarters area. He knew if one nail was missing from a corral corner or if a hinge lacked a single bolt from a building door. Such was the Patrón, a person who did not tolerate waste or haste. On his walks, he carried a cane with a magnetic horseshoe, and all stray nails, bolts would attach to it. These he would save. For to preach to your workers, he felt must include the preacher...he practiced what he preached.

Doña Pablita sometimes could not fully understand Don José's ways because it seemed such a change from her own philosophy of life. She stayed busy with her children. Already Don José had mentioned that the education of the growing children would soon have to be dealt with. The small school in Galisteo did not provide the educational opportunities Don José wanted for his children, so he had discussed the possibility of buying a winter home in Santa Fe. Pablita could move there with the children in order for them to attend better schools. Doña Pablita did not care too much for the idea, but in a way it was the best solution. Don José would go to Santa Fe twice a week to be with them. There was also the possibility of boarding the children at one of the two religious schools in Santa Fe. Doña Pablita felt she would like to start with boarding the children and see how that worked. If it did not work well, she would move to town.

Don José and Doña Pablita loved their beautiful home in Galisteo which they had planned so carefully. It was constructed of adobe blocks and the roof was galvanized sheeting which had been ordered from the East. The house contained eight rooms and had several porches. The kitchen was large and airy. It looked out toward the orchards which were growing well and bearing fruit. The rooms were furnished in good taste by Doña Pablita with fine oak and maple furniture from New England, and scattered about were heavy Spanish and Mexican pieces that had been in both their families for generations. Navajo and old Rio Grande rugs from Chimayo served as floor covering. Tapestries and shawls from Spain adorned the walls. There was a fireplace in each room. It was no wonder Doña Pablita hesitated to leave her home.

Don José heard from one of his political friends in Santa Fe that a great tract of land close to the village of Palma would soon be opened up for homesteading. He immediately investigated this good news, for he had often admired this parcel of land. His father had taken him to this area many times to trade and to visit old friends. It was not that far from Galisteo, only about forty miles to the southeast as the crow flies. The possibility that this rich and well-watered land could be stocked with thousands more sheep and cattle challenged him. His holdings already totaled some 50,000 acres in the Galisteo area, but this parcel which the old settlers called *agua verde* (green water), totaled some 150,000 acres. It would be hard work and he would have to learn this new land. If he could settle it and finally acquire it, his dream of becoming the largest landowner in the State would be close to realization. His son, Frank, was growing fast and soon would be able to help. Don José would pray for this.

"Valentino, please come in the office," Don José asked one morning.

"Yes, Patrón!"

"Frank will soon be going to school in Santa Fe with the Christian Brothers. But he will be here every weekend and every chance he gets.

So, when he comes in the store, try to teach him something about the books or sales. Try to familiarize him with the operation of the store and the cantina."

"Yes, Patrón. I will be most happy to do so. Frank is a smart boy. He will catch on fast," Valentino answered with a broad smile.

As they were talking, the store door bell rang. Valentino peered out, then went to the door. A stranger was there. The man asked for Don José.

"I'm Don José, Señor," he said as he extended his hand in greeting.

"I am Robert Seligman from Boston, Massachusetts," the gentleman replied. "I am a wool buyer and owner of a large warehouse in Boston."

Don José asked him into the office and pulled a chair up for him. "What brings you out this way, Señor Seligman?"

"I want to talk business with you, as we are aware that you control one of the largest herds of sheep in New Mexico," he answered.

"Yes, that is true, but you come from so far, and most of our wool production is sold to buyers here in New Mexico."

"Señor, we would like to buy wool direct and have it shipped by rail from Lamy. We would also like to utilize your services as a buyer. Perhaps you would think about building a small warehouse here in Galisteo where you could store your wool and your neighbors' – and anyone else's you could buy. We are in need of wool, Don José, since the European market is creating a heavy demand on our other sources."

"Señor Seligman, I am presently increasing my herds, and to me this sounds like a good proposition. You may consider it done! We can discuss it at greater length at lunch," Don José told him.

Don José felt the time was right for such a transaction and later that day after Mr. Seligman's departure, he called in his carpenter. "Juan, I want a large building constructed from stone, with good ventilation and wooden floors. I want to use it to store sacks of wool."

"Yes, Don José. And where shall we build it?" Juan asked.

"East of the stables, close to the alameda on the river front."

"I will get the men together and start tomorrow."

It was another challenge for Don José but he felt this would pro-vide more income; yet more importantly, he would be able to meet more people and controlling large quantities of wool would enable him to get a better price for his and his people's wool. Until then, they almost always took what the local dealers offered. Many of his friends and homesteaders were losing money on their wool.

Sylvester Davis had been dead for some time now, and Doña Josefita had been having trouble with her eyesight. Doña Pablita was spending a great deal of time helping her mother with the housework at her huge hacienda. Of course, there were the faithful Jade and others, but to maintain this hacienda had become a burden after Sylvester died. Prior to his passing away, Sylvester had petitioned for a patent that included the hacienda and one hundred sixty acres, taking in all the center of the village. He had been granted the patent and these lands had to be cared for. Sylvester and Doña Josefita had allowed many villagers to build homes on the land but they never gave them deeds for the land.

Don José was very fond of Doña Josefita and would send her meat and other things he knew she liked from his store. Little did he know that someday the huge hacienda would be his.

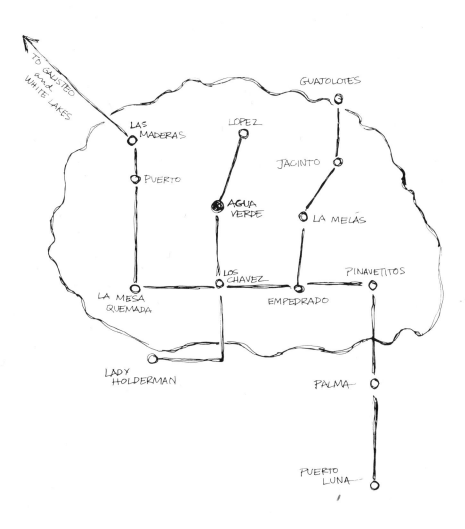

five

Don José planned a trip to Palma for he wanted to study the land he was going to acquire and to meet the people of the area. He would have to be careful because this land was a very desolate part of the State and only a few people lived scattered throughout this vast tract. Don José arrived in Palma and visited with the Tenorio family. He was treated as all guests were, like family by these kind and gentle people. They chatted late into the night. Don José told them of his plan and he asked that the word go out he would be willing to offer sheep, cattle and a good price for the land when it was sold to him.

Don José realized a tract this large would almost have to be treated like a new country. *Agua Verde* would be a state within a state. He would have to establish a few small settlements so there would be enough people to help run this vast empire, just like Galisteo served as the hub of his holdings in the Galisteo Basin.

He had taken with him an old friend and storyteller, Porfidio Hurtado. His stories were colorful and endless. Don José knew the people in these small villages considered storytelling one of their main forms of entertainment.

"Let's see," Porfidio said. "I have a strange story about a *curandero* whom the *brujas* did not like because he was always undoing their evil work. I think I will tell you of Juanito and his magical ways and also about his home."

"We will all enjoy that *cuento*, Porfidio," Don José said.

"But first, another cup of *mula*, my friends! And gather close so I don't have to shout," Porfidio said with a big grin. He did enjoy entertaining with his storytelling.

"First, let me tell you about where Juanito lived. It was a long ride or walk to the foot of the Ortiz Mountains where Juanito, the *brujo*, had his small, two-room adobe, which nestled amongst a grove of piñon trees. As you approached it from the north you could see his view was panoramic down toward the beautiful basins that lay to the east and north. His home was very much like an eagle's nest and from it he could observe every movement that took place in the enormous valley below.

"His home was made in the old manner of rock and mud. There were two rooms: a kitchen and a small room which he called his temple. As you entered Juanito's kitchen – since this was the only door to the small home – you noticed nothing really out of the ordinary. There was an old fireplace in which he cooked, various types of cooking utensils scattered here and there and a pot of beans in the hot coals which he was preparing for his daily meal. An old hand-hewn table occupied the center of the small kitchen and beside it were a couple of ancient chairs. A small inverted cross was painted over one of the windows. A plant or two lazily reflected the rays of the morning sunshine in the window, while his aged cat lay snug in front of the fireplace on an old sheepskin. A piece of jerked mutton always hung from one of the vigas over his table, as Juanito had his own small herd of sheep he grazed at the foot of the mountains he called home. There were no pictures on the walls except for a few of his sketches which he had done with pieces of burnt wood. These were of birds, a deer, a mountain lion, perhaps a bear – all animals he had encountered – done in his own abstract way. His kitchen was used strictly for preparing and eating his meals.

"Now upon entering the room he called his temple, there was another sight for it was in this room where Juanito lived, studied and helped people. Here was a room fashioned so everything he needed for his various rituals in contacting the spiritual world was handily available to him. Against one wall was a small, wooden bunkbed with sheep pelts and multicolored blankets cast upon it which Juanito wove from his sheep's wool on a small loom. They were dyed with the natural vegetable dyes he collected. The one window in the room served as his altar. Underneath the window was a small table which was filled with many partially burned candles, and scattered amongst them were small cheesecloth bags which you could make out to be filled with various types of dried herbs, dried bones and perhaps internal organs of different animals. There were also a few cutting utensils, various crucibles and a small burner improvised from a candle – all of which he used to mix various potions in the art of *brujeria* (witchcraft). On the ceiling, suspended from the vigas, were hundreds of small bags like many of those lying on the altar. They, too, contained herbs and various materials used by Juanito in his art. His altar had a small stool in front of it, and the floor was covered with sheep pelts. Above the window was a big black cross inverted, and on all the walls were a series of other inverted black crosses. The only illumination that would come into this room at night would be candlelight or, if he was fortunate, from a small, kerosene lamp.

"This was Juanito's temple. This was the place where people would come to seek help. Here he would practice his art. Here the many secrets of years and years of study by him and what had been passed down to him by his forefathers, would take place in the art of contacting the spirits from another world. There were no pictures of saints in this room, and no pictures of the devil or evil spirits, for Juanito's strength lay in the fact that his art was an art of contacting spirits – spirits much like his would be someday – spirits who could give him great knowledge and great strength to perform the art of *brujería* when it was needed.

"Leaving the adobe building, one saw travelers approaching from the north.The next part of the story that unfolds is about a visit to Juanito's temple. The name of it is, 'The Ball of Barbed Wire.'

Porfidio's audience didn't stir from its seat, but urged him, "Go on with the story!" Someone refreshed his cup of *mula* and he continued:

"Doña Valencia had been ill for a number of months. Her stomach and her entire body were swollen out of proportion. She had not been able to eat a meal for over a month now. She had not been able to drink any type of liquid except very small quantities of water. There was great concern amongst Doña Valencia's family. The medico, the old *curandero* of a nearby area, had done all the herbal magic he could possibly do as far as medicinal treatment was concerned. Now things began to get worse, so the long trek to Juanito's temple was in order. Not being able to travel on foot, a wagon was prepared and readied by Arturo, the husband of the sick woman, and they set out in search of the *brujo*.

"On the way to the foot of the mountains where the *brujo* lived, Doña Valencia kept telling her husband she felt what people in the village were saying – that she'd been *embrujada* (bewitched) – was correct. She knew if anyone could help her, Juanito could, if this were the truth.

She had had a run-in with an old *bruja* many, many years before. The *bruja* had warned her she would become very ill and pay for the run-in they had. At the time Doña Valencia, being a strong woman, had laughed it off and paid no attention to the threat.

"But recently, she noticed for a number of months that a little grandchild of the old *bruja* had occasionally brought her soup and little stews to share at her home. Doña Valencia had accepted them willingly and partaken of them with the child. Now, she was telling her husband, Arturo, 'Perhaps in this food the child's grandmother has bewitched me. Maybe the food has made me ill. I feel close to the point of death. Only Juanito will know if there is any way I can dissolve this witchcraft that overpowers me.'

"As they approached Juanito's house, they hollered to him. Juanito gave his greeting in return and asked them to enter. They dismounted from the wagon and Arturo brought his frail wife in with Juanito's help. In the small kitchen, Juanito served them a cup of manzanilla tea, better known as camomille. As they talked and visited, Juanito studied Doña Valencia's eyes and her body, and then went into a semi-trance as she spoke and told him of her beliefs of what had happened and why.

"After listening to her explain the things that had been going on with her during these months of her great illness, Juanito asked Arturo for permission to touch Doña Valencia's stomach. Arturo nodded his consent. The *brujo* placed his left hand on Doña Valencia's stomach near the navel and began to rub in a circular motion. He got to one particular area to the right of the navel and stopped. Juanito looked at Arturo and Doña Valencia and said, 'I think we know what I must do. The day has much light left yet. We shall go outside and prepare for the evening.' With that Juanito took Doña Valencia gently by the hand, and with Arturo's help placed her in a sunny spot in the front patio of his little home and asked her to relax. He also asked Arturo to sit by her and not bother him for he would be very busy there in their presence. Juanito then excused himself and went back into the temple. From the ceiling he removed a bag that was filled with black horsehair which had been cut from the tail or mane. He took the hair back out to the sunny area and sat on an old bench and began to weave a very fine, thin rope. He worked on it for two hours and all the while did not exchange a word with his visitors.

"At last he was finished. He beckoned to Doña Valencia. He said, 'Now you must follow me. Come with me. Arturo, with your permission you will wait here for us while we go inside. Maybe we will have an answer to your wife's illness soon.'

"Juanito and Doña Valencia then went into the temple. Juanito placed on the altar the rope of horsehair he had woven so delicately and finely. It was about five feet long. A few candles were lit. Then he motioned for Doña Valencia to sit on one of the sheepskins on the floor. 'Please say some prayers. Pray in any way you want and pray to whomever you wish. I will be with you in a moment.'

"Juanito started his ritual. The candles that were ignited were repositioned on his altar. He removed various powders and dusts from some of the crucibles and these were sprinkled on the horsehair rope. He reached for another small bag. It contained small fish bones. Out of one, he fashioned a type of small hook – it was minute in size – and attached it to the horsehair rope. Then he covered the rope with a buttery substance...only he knew what it was. Juanito recited a few chants before he took a big bag fashioned and woven out of wool and placed the rope in it, then approached Doña Valencia. As he knelt next to her he said, 'You must not yell. You must trust me. You must get well and I will make you well.'

"She answered, 'I trust you, Juanito. And more than anything, I wish to recover from this illness.'

" 'Then lie on your back on the sheepskin, Doña Valencia,' he said as he pulled the rope from the bag. He annointed her head with a powder he had been mixing and told her, 'Now close your eyes and swallow ...very slowly...swallow the rope as I put it in your mouth.' He inserted the rope into her mouth and gently guided it into her stomach. When most of the horsehair rope had entered her, he said, 'Stop!' Then he did other bits of ritual in his own words, in his own dialogue, and at that moment there was a great strength that came over him. Doña Valencia felt a great relief coming over her. Juanito then started to slowly pull the rope out again and finally – at the end of it – emerged a ball about the size of an egg. As he removed it from her mouth Doña Valencia coughed once or twice, shivered and shuddered, then fell into a deep sleep.

"Juanito took the ball he had removed from her stomach and placed it on his altar. On doing so, the ball started to expand in size. It grew to the size of an orange. It was a ball of barbed wire. Juanito grabbed it carefully and put it inside one of his cheesecloth bags. He stood and said a few other words, then went over to Doña Valencia and tapped her gently. 'Wake! It is done. We must go out and see your husband.'

"They went outdoors to Arturo, who by this time was very nervous. Doña Valencia flung herself into his arms joyfully. She cried out, 'I am so hungry! Juanito, those beans you have cooking smell so good. May I have some? And some tortillas? Oh, I can never thank you enough!'

" 'And I thank you, Juanito!' Arturo beamed in gratitude.

" 'Before we celebrate,' Juanito said, 'I must tell you what you had in you.' He removed the ball of barbed wire from the cheesecloth bag. Arturo and Valencia stood in disbelief. 'This was in you; this was placed in you by the *bruja* who bewitched you. It came to you in the meals her grandchild brought you. She started it with small slivers of metal and she kept putting them in your food until finally until finally it became a ball. She would have succeeded in killing you. But now we have removed it. So! We shall eat and rejoice that the spirits have granted us the power to make you well.'

"They passed the evening talking, then went to their beds. As the morning sun came out of the east, Juanito bade Arturo and Doña Valencia farewell and asked them to give his regards to the villagers and said, 'If you believe, Señora, Eternity will always ride by your side.'

All in the gathering were spellbound. "One more *cuento*, Porfidio! You really are a fine storyteller," they said.

"Thank you, my friends," he answered. "Perhaps when you visit Galisteo one of these days, I will tell you another story."

Once morning arrived, Don José said goodbye to his hosts and reminded them again of his offer. "I will wait a month and see how many of you are interested." Then he and Porfidio, who drove the wagon-type carriage, started out to discover this new land.

A road led directly northeast of Palma across the northern boundary of this great area. A few miles from Palma, they came upon a small house and corral. Living there was a Señor Trujillo who advised them that he was formally homesteading a hundred sixty acres. Don José asked if there were others homesteading within *Agua Verde*. Señor Trujillo told him that only two other families were. Don José was relieved to hear this and realized he had come not any too soon. Don José told Señor Trujillo about his plan and that he was sure they would be good neighbors.

It took almost three days for them to ride *Agua Verde*. How vast and great this land was, with beautiful valleys, rolling hills, healthy piñon scrub, canyons with huge pine trees and beautiful running springs "A blending that truly God had taken special pains in planning," Don José thought.

With every turn there was a new sight. Already Don José was mapping out trails and roads and areas for small settlements. He could tell by the vegetation and land erosion that more rain and snow fell here than in the Galisteo Basin. He started to name valleys and high points and drew a small map as they traveled along. They came across a few more people who were living on the land and again Don José treated them kindly and with respect. He repeated his plan to all of them.

As they left from the south boundary on the return trip home, he mentioned to Porfidio, "I will start with some of our people from the village to homestead this land. On our return, I will determine how many families this vast area needs to settle it all."

The trip had done much for Don José's spiritual and physical needs. He could plainly feel and sense the boldness and courage of his forefathers as they arrived in this new and mysterious land a couple of centuries before. "Still, there is so much land to love and make come alive," he thought. "My forefathers barely scratched the surface of this territory. I will develop this land and make it the finest ranch in the state Here vast herds of sheep and cattle will roam, and here I will realize my dream."

There was so much to do when he arrived at his headquarters. Everyone wanted to talk to him and report to him at the same time. Pablita told him how she and the children had missed him and other news which always seemed to happen whenever he was away for a day or two. Travelers and neighbors were waiting to see him, even a few people who wanted to go out and homestead his new country. A new clerk was needed, for old Valentino was ill. Everywhere he went, all he heard made him feel he had been away for a year. This was his life – he was involved in so many things and his projects grew instead of slowing down. He needed help badly. Soon his son would be ready to assume his responsibilities. "Then I'll be able to rest, at least a little," he thought as he smiled to himself.

The wool warehouse was finished and already neighbors and friends whom Don José had contacted were starting to bring their wool. Fall was on its way and the men could feel the tempo of the Patrón's demands, for when this season arrived, there was much to do in order to prepare for winter.

The herds of sheep and cattle would all be gathered and then sorting would take place. Also, the livestock would be moved to winter areas. Buyers would soon be arriving to barter with Don José. He loved this part of his life. The livestock buyers were a challenge for him, since those who came to Galisteo were the best in the business. Sometimes the buyers would come out a little ahead and other times Don José would win, but all this bargaining was done in a spirit of friendship and respect.

Don José would help his neighbors draw up sales contracts and help them sell their livestock together with his. He never dickered with his people, for he knew their needs. If anything, he would give them what price they asked and more often, a little more.

Respect for Don José grew and most of the villagers felt secure with the presence of their Patrón. Many had been friends of his father, Don Juan, and as they looked at Don José they remarked, "Don Juan was a great Patrón and loved the people, but Don José is closer to his people and moves much faster than Don Juan. He truly cares about his dedication, but he never steps on anyone to achieve it."

Don José walked across the street to see Doña Josefita for he had picked many herbs for her on his trip to *Agua Verde*. After greeting each other, he presented her with oregano *del campo* (wild oregano), manzanilla or camomille and various other herbs he knew would be useful in her role as a *curandera* or native doctor.

Doña Josefita had helped many people with her knowledge of medicinal herbs which she had learned from her mother. During these early years doctors were rare in these rural areas and it was up to people like Doña Josefita to care for the health needs of whoever came to her. This was knowledge and power that could not be abused. Nor was there a fee, for money could not pass hands if a cure was to be obtained.

She was the best and was well-respected by all who sought her medicine. Doña Josefita cared for expectant mothers as well as delivered their babies. She was called upon to instruct people to prepare the dead for burial. She attended the people from the cradle to the grave and in between...neckaches, backaches, broken bones, even a "hot" appendix, these and many more cures could she effect. Don José went to her many times when he only needed to talk, for her power was magical, even in conversation. She was going blind, but the handicap did not stop her many endeavors. The only thing she could no longer do was ride horses.

Don José's children were ready for further schooling, and he and Pablita had decided she would move to Santa Fe so the children could acquire a better education. Frank did not like the idea of being away from his father very much as Don José took Frank with him wherever he went. Don José wanted him to learn the land, the people and, most of all, the affairs of his business. No matter what he was transacting, Don José would have Frank sit with him in the office and listen. Don José felt a man could learn what books could not teach. So, with the separation, Don José would miss Frank's daily presence, but he knew they would be together every chance they could.

The *Agua Verde* acquisition was coming along well, and what land Don José was not homesteading, he was acquiring piece by piece from others who had slowly started to move into the land. His business was beginning to feel the supply and demand problems caused by World War I. A few villagers and good friends from the area had enlisted in order to participate in the Great War. Don José knew that his work would keep him in Galisteo. The thought of serving in the Army did fascinate him but only during his secret moments with himself. Things would have to change now that he was in the big house alone. Doña Pablita came often to clean and freshen the house and she and the children could hardly wait until Don José travelled to Santa Fe to spend weekends with them.

He had more hours of the day to fill with work since his family was away, and thus his drive and supervision of his holdings became more intense. Don José was fortunate to have some very special men as his *caporales* or foremen. There was a *caporal* for the sheep, one for the cattle, another for his headquarters-workers, and still another for the people who were homesteading. So very much depended on these faithful and hardworking foremen. They would report to the Patrón every evening and morning of the year.

Don José daily performed his ritual of pounding a log after he awoke early each morning. By six o'clock, one could hear throughout the village the *cencerro* or cow bell that was rung to announce the morning meal. The cooks, of course, were up as early as Don José, getting the breakfast ready. They fed two shifts of twelve men each. These were the men who actually lived around the headquarters. The workers who lived in the village usually had their meals in their homes, but they also could partake of the good, wholesome meals that Don José insisted his cooks prepare.

Hearing the *cencerro*, the men would wait for their Patrón to arrive before they filed into the dining room. A long table, seating twelve people, was in the center of the room. Along the walls were hooks for the men to hang their jackets and hats. Don José sat at the head of the table. One noticed his place had a china place setting and a small tablecloth. The other places were set with tin plates and cups with only spoons as silverware. There was always a pitcher of fresh milk and a big pot of coffee. The cooks would fill the plates for the men. Breakfast varied, but always there were fresh biscuits or tortillas, as many eggs as you could eat and either red or green chili.

Don José would have the *caporales*, the storekeeper and cantina clerk sit with him on the first shift. He always finished eating first since he was served first, and then he would spend the rest of the mealtime giving instructions to his main force of men. After the meal he would retire to the store with his 'brain-trust' to continue with the work orders for the day. When the rest of the men had finished eating, everyone was ready to start the workday. Men who would be riding long distances during that day would have a lunch packed for them.

Every single phase of Don José's operation was well planned and his men found it easy to work for him, for his orders and plans were always made absolutely clear to the *caporales*, and they in turn made the orders clear to the men under them. All the seasons had their peculiar changes and adjustments, but life never got boring working for the Patrón. Don José was now providing work for most of the villagers and as he developed *Agua Verde* there would be need for more men.

Times were good in Galisteo. People were happy and most of them employed. Those who did not work for the Patrón raised a few crops and had a few animals, worked for the railroad or traveled throughout the State and Southern Colorado as sheepherders. The women of the village were always busy with their household chores and raising their families. In the village the people were devout Catholics and large families abounded. There was no time for idleness in Galisteo. The smallest child had responsibility – hauling water, carrying wood for the stoves. The older children would work in the fields or help their mothers plaster their homes, for the adobes had to be mud plastered at least once a year. The homes were small and simple, but kept very clean. Each family prided itself on the cleanliness and appearance of the family dwelling. The poorest person had a place to stay. No one was ever turned away. No one ever went hungry, for if he ran out of food or money, there was always the Patrón. Don José had his clerk keep a large ledger where food items and loans were recorded which would be paid back in work for the Patrón or whenever someone had money to pay some amount on his account. There was no such thing as interest or carrying charges and the food items that were bought at Don José's were marked up only five per cent. He made his money from the volume of business and from the people working out their bills. The same was true of the cantina. Don José knew his men would drink somewhere, so why not with him?

It was remarkable the way the system worked. No one ever ran out on Don José without settling his debts – for he would always return to Galisteo – and in time, Don José would approach him with a job, whether it was cleaning the corrals, chopping wood or a million other things only the Patrón could think up.

People respected each other and discrimination, for all practical purposes, was unheard of. The Anglo or *gringo* was respected and admired by most of the Spanish settlers. A funny, but true, comment was often heard when you saw a woman with a baby talking to another woman. Almost invariably the woman wishing to complement the mother with child would comment, "*¡Qué bonito, parece gringito!*" (How beautiful. He looks like a gringo!) It was an honest statement by the woman. There was no time for discrimination in this country at this period in history. Survival depended on cooperation with everyone. Of course, as in every herd of white sheep, there are a few black ones and such in every village. There were characters who did not get along with anybody – much less themselves.

Feast days of patron saints and other festive occasions were a time of celebration. The people prepared well for these. On one feast day in particular, *El Día de San Juan*, which came in early summer, the village went all out: they held a rodeo, rooster-pulls, there was racing and entertainers were brought in – these were called *payasos* or clowns. *Maromeros* or tumblers were another attraction. Festivities of all kinds were held during the day and finally topped off by a big *baile* or dance at night. The revelry continued until early morning, and then it was peace and quiet until the next St. John's Day.

Galisteo: Día de San Juan, St. John's Day, chicken pull.

six

World War I was over. Don José had nearly concluded his settling of *Agua Verde* and Frank had almost completed his schooling. He soon would be spending all his time with his father. As events would have it, with an increase in the Patrón's power, the political world on the local level demanded Don José's leadership. A delegation of local politicians was ushered into his office one summer day. They were there to ask him to run for County Commissioner. He did not need this extra responsibility but it was a challenge and challenges nourished him. After a lengthy meeting, he agreed to run and it was no surprise that Don José won by a large margin of votes.

The political system somehow reminded him of his own business methods: favors would have to be repaid with favors. Don José could see great benefits emanating from this new position, for he and his people needed roads, bridges, fencing and a voice about property taxes. He set out to try to make the position productive...and he did. It also enabled him to place more people of Galisteo in jobs.

He served two terms and then the political power in the area needed him in the State Legislature. When approached with this subject, he decided to wait to run for his empire could not wait. It was growing fast and with it came a more concentrated demand on his time. But Don José was ready for *Agua Verde* – and so was his "star." Frank had finished his schooling. The Christian Brothers had nothing but praise for him as a student...he had been a leader in his class and had excelled in mathematics.

Don José was proud of his son's achievements and immediately told him, "Frank, your chair is ready. You will help me build the largest sheep and cattle ranch in the area. We have much to do, but we will do it side by side."

"Papa, I will help you and be by your side, for my dream has always been to help you," Frank replied. And thus began a relationship that would be the envy of all fathers and sons, a relationship based on love and complete trust.

Don José assigned Frank complete charge of all the bookwork. Frank would also supervise all the *caporales* and *mayordomos* and in the future they would report to him.

Doña Pablita remained in Santa Fe with the other children while Frank moved in with his father at the Galisteo house.

Automobiles and trucks were rapidly becoming widespread and the Patrón began to acquire these unusual creations of eastern America. These vehicles would serve to bring his land holdings closer together and distance would now be of little consequence

Don José always dressed elegantly, usually in grey or light brown vested suits. He wore a tie, a wide brimmed Stetson and usually smoked a big cigar. He would set out early in the morning with Frank for the *Agua Verde*. Don José never cared to drive so Frank was the chauffeur. As they left the outskirts of the village, a rosary was started. Don José would recite the first part and Frank would do the answering. Two rosaries were prayed before they would arrive at the entrance of *Agua Verde*. The Patrón would always tell his son and his people, "*Dios por delante!* Place God ahead of your work." And this be believed and lived by. "Always pray, and instead of just asking all the time, try and thank God for what you already have," he preached to Frank.

Entering the vast expanse of *Agua Verde* the road led to the first settlement which was called Los Chavez, named after a family Don José had living there. Los Chavez had a big, beautiful water tank and a fine set of corrals. Within walking distance of them was a cluster of three houses and various sheds. Here lived one of Don José's *caporales* Señor Ambrosio Chavez, a most versatile man – good with sheep and cattle. Los Chavez was also used as a lambing and shearing station. The view from Los Chavez was magnificent: in every direction was a pristine wilderness – rolling hills and long valleys covered with lush grama grass, a painter's delight of wildflowers, an abundance of herbs of various families flourishing and, in the distance, the occasional smoke from the dwelling of a homesteader. The ranch was circled to the south and west by splendid mesas and timber country and to the east and south by low-lying valleys and rolling hills.

After Don José and Frank visited with Señor Chavez, they received a food and feed order from him. The sheepherders under his care would leave their need-orders for El Patrón which Ambrosio would deliver weekly when Don José and Frank came by. The orders were filled and delivered from Galisteo by one of the Patrón's trucks within two days. In time, Don José and Frank would set up a central well-stocked commissary which made it easier for all their people to acquire their needs.

Lambing time was imminent and the excitement of the event kept father and son in constant conversation as they left Los Chavez and headed southeast toward another settlement which they called Empedrado, the rock area. Here there was a great earthen and rock dam and living on the edge of it was the family of Señor Miguel Romero, a family who years later would play an important part in New Mexico's religious history. Miguel Romero was a favorite worker of the Patrón's. His family all worked for Don José and, as he and Frank arrived in front of their house, the family came out to greet them.

"Buenos días, Patrón!" called Miguel.

"Buenos días, mi buen amigo!" answered Don José.

After exchanging greetings and presenting Miguel with a beautiful pair of gloves from his store, Don José and Frank sat on the bank of the huge dam and discussed the lambing period. "Will all your family be willing to help again this year?" Don José asked. Miguel assured them they would and were looking forward to the lambing as much as El Patrón was. Lambing time was special. It always brought the people from the settlements in *Agua Verde* together and when the day's work was done, news and stories were exchanged.

The Patrón gazed up toward a small hill behind Miguel's house and, as always, noticed the lonely but beautifully-carved cross standing there. He knew that Miguel was very active in the Penitente Brotherhood. The Penitentes were a religious organization which was associated with the Catholic Church but was constantly at odds with the Church because of the rituals used to commemorate the crucifixion of Christ. The rituals during Miguel's time called for the actual crucifixion of a selected Brother. The man selected to be crucified on Good Friday was highly respected and honored.

The religious ceremony took place in the Penitentes' morada, or chapel, during Holy Week. The ceremonies and rituals culminated on Good Friday with the crucifixion. The Catholic Church did not condone this and for a period of time actually excommunicated the Brotherhood. It would not be until the 1950s when the Church and the Brotherhood would settle their differences. At that time, Miguel Romero would be the leader, the Supreme Brother of the Penitentes throughout Northern New Mexico. On this day he was only a Brother sitting with his Patrón.

Don José respected Miguel. The Patrón had an innate ability to judge people: he could sense their past, their present and their future, and this knowledge enabled him to build up his empire. His understanding way with people was repaid with loyalty and dedication from all those who worked for him – in addition to the love they felt for him. Miguel was one such person employed by Don José. And Don José knew instinctively all along that some day Miguel's future held greatness in his religious endeavor.

Now everywhere he went, seeing about his lands and business, Don José carried with him a black leather bag. It contained every patent medicine he could order through his store as well as a great variety of medicinal herbs. This bag was regarded as magical by the people – as was Don José by many – for there were no doctors in this area and all healing was in the hands of people such as he who had some knowledge of the human body and its responses both to herbs and to patent medicines.

It happened that one of Miguel's children had been having a persistant stomach problem. "Would you be so kind to reach into your bag and see if you have anything that will help my child, Don José?" Miguel requested. After listening to the father relate the child's symptoms, Don José took out a bottle of *aceite Mejicano* and instructed Miguel in its use. He also left some herbs for the child.

Frank listed the articles of Miguel's need-order before they left. "I will see you on our next trip, Miguel. By that time plans should be set for the lambing date," Don José called and off he and Frank went, toward the largest settlement in *Agua Verde*, called La Melás, the syrup.

On the way they came across a sheep camp nestled in a pine grove not far from the road. They would try to visit as many of the herds of sheep and camps as possible on their trips to *Agua Verde* but because the area was so vast and held many places which were inaccessible to their vehicle, they were prevented from seeing them all. So it was they would check with the *mayordomos* and *caporales* at the various settlements in order to stay well versed on the condition of their herds. Around this time the sheep in *Agua Verde* numbered close to 50,000 head. Galisteo lands were grazing around 10,000 head. Their cattle numbered close to 2,000 in both areas. As they drove up to this sheep camp they were greeted by Luis Chavez and talked with him for fifteen minutes or so. While discussing the business affairs, Frank noticed some *carne seca*, jerky, hanging from a limb of a nearby tree. This was a treat both he and Don José looked forward to eating when they visited one of the sheep camps. They would each eat a few pieces there and then, in a gentle way, would take half of it back to Galisteo. The camper would kill another sheep and make more, always happy the jerky pleased his Patrón. Don José's men were allowed to kill as many of the old, fat ewes as they needed for their meals.

Each sheep camp consisted of the *pastor*, sheepherder, and the *campero*, camper. The *pastor* was directly responsible for the herd under his care. Each herd usually numbered between 800 and 1,000 head. Some of the herds were made up of ewes and lambs while other herds were composed of yearlings. Then there were herds of rams. A good *pastor* could pretty well handle any type of herd. He was the boss and was over the camper. The camper's duty was to move the camp from one place to another and he was responsible for providing three meals a day for the pastor and himself. Under the camper's care was a group of six or seven burros which carried the camp gear when they changed location. These burros were well trained and when the camp was in place they were hobbled and let loose to graze. The leader of the burro herd had a large cowbell tied around his neck so the camper could always locate him. When the *pastor* determined his herd needed better grass he would order the camper to scout a new camp area in better grass country. Preparing to move the camp, the camper would disassemble the tent and pack all the foodstuffs and other wares in large wooden boxes. These boxes were in turn tied to the pack saddles on the burros. Prior to placing the pack-saddles on the burros' backs, sheep-skins were placed on their backs, then the saddles. These sheepskins served as carpeting in the tent each time it was set up.

Before Don José and Frank left, Luis Chavez called for the magical black bag. "I have a bad toothache, Patrón. Do you have a remedy, perhaps?"

Don José pulled out a box of cloves and handed them to Luis with a few instructions. "Boil these in water and gargle with the liquid; then push a piece of the soft, cooked clove into the tooth cavity or close to the hurting area. If this doesn't work, have the *pastor* pull it out for you."

Luis thanked them and Don José and Frank headed toward Melás. Already the sun was high and they had not been able to visit some of the herds they had hoped to see. They knew Manuel Chavez would be waiting for them at Melás with a complete report of all the sheep and cattle herds. He was their main *mayordomo* in *Agua Verde*, in charge of their largest settlement as well as the whole ranch at *Agua Verde*. He and the Patrón had been together a long time. Manuel's family was large and all the members held the Patrón in great esteem. The entire family felt secure in their relationship with the Patrón and none had any desire to leave his employ. He provided them with a good life. People from larger towns might ridicule them and say, "You are like slaves there with your patrón!" But Manuel and the others knew better. Don José respected them and appreciated their work. He praised them when praise was due and he scolded them when a reprimand was in order. They had homes and their own livestock. They lacked nothing. In fact, their needs were taken care of far better than those of the big-town peo-ple, and there is little doubt the people from the larger towns would have traded places with them in a minute. Certainly the Patrón was demanding, but he was also giving.

As they approached La Melás which was situated at the end of a lovely valley and at the beginning of a large canyon, Don José remarked, "My son, this has to be the most beautiful area of *Agua Verde!*"

"Papa, why don't we build a house here so we can come and spend a few days...At least have more time to see all the men?" Frank asked.

Don José like the idea. He would start planning the building on their return to Galisteo. As they neared the settlement, a huge bulk of a man appeared in front of one of the larger houses. It was none other than Manuel. He greeted his Patrón. Already he respected Frank. Manuel was wise and he could feel Frank would follow in Don José's footsteps.

"Patrón! You both must be hungry. Come in. My wonderful wife has a good lunch for you," Manuel said.

The men entered the clean and well-kept home and were greeted by Manuel's exact opposite – a petite, attractive woman who was Manuel's mainstay. After greeting Manuel's gracious wife, Don José was offered a cup of coffee and escorted to their table. For El Patrón, they had a special plate and cup. Frank also received special treatment. They were served a wonderful meal of *cabrito* (roasted kid) and pinto beans with, of course, homemade bread. For desert was fabulous *arroz con pasas* (rice with raisins), a favorite pudding of Don José's. After the meal, the three men walked out and sat under Señor Manuel's favorite piñon tree.

Manuel felt proud to be sitting with his Patrón as he answered all the questions about the condition of the livestock. Don José always asked about Manuel's people, what was happening in their lives and about their health. An hour went by so fast! Manuel had not finished his report.

Don José advised Manuel of his decision to build a house for himself and Frank so they could stay particularly during lambing and branding time but also whenever time would allow them to be at *Agua Verde*. He also discussed building a commissary there so all the campers could replenish their supplies whenever necessary.

Señor Chavez' smaller children played around the tree while the men visited and the younger girls of the family would peek out at them now and then from behind a door or window. They cared very much for Frank and the Patrón and were always curious to see them when they arrived. Women at this time were still very sheltered. They were taught to keep their distance and hold their tongues when the family had visitors. One would think that it would have been impossible for young ladies in remote settlements to ever find husbands. However this was not the case, as a considerable number of young men would gather during lambing, shearing and branding time. Branding time was an especially fine opportunity for the young bucks to prove their *macho*!

Young ladies were permitted to go to the corral area with their mothers or other older ladies to observe the men rope and bulldog the wild cattle. Truly these cattle were a test, for the ranch was so vast that sometimes new calves never saw a *vaquero* until roundup time for branding.

Young men also worked as sheepherders and campers and from time to time would visit all the settlements – on one kind of business or another. Looking for eligible young ladies to marry was certainly an important aspect of their lives!

As the three men said goodbye to each other, a *vaquero* rode up on his marvelous cowpony. *"Buenos días, Patrón."* he greeted.

"Buenos días, mi hijito." Don José answered. All through his life he continued to greet and call his men *hijito. ¿Qué pasa?"* he asked.

"I've found six dead cows on the north side of the ranch close to the settlement called Jacinto," the cowboy answered.

"Were they shot, or did it appear some animal killed them? Or did they died of a disease?" Don José asked.

"I think they died from eating a poisonous weed, Señor."

This was one the the everyday problems Manuel faced. He told the young *vaquero* he would go with him to see about the cows as soon as the Patrón left. "We will move the cattle out of that area. Get three more hands to help us."

Manuel was a most competent man and Don José always had complete faith in his ability. After taking Manuel's need-order and more goodbyes, Don José and Frank headed toward Galisteo. As they left the ranch entrance and had traveled a few miles on the highway home, Don José suggested, "Let's stop and have a refreshment with our good friend Mrs. Halderman." Frank did not have to be asked twice. He always enjoyed having a glass of brandy and listening to the latest news in the area which Mrs. Halderman always seemed to know. They parked in front of the building which housed her service station, bar and store. As they walked in Mrs. Halderman appeared from behind one of the buildings. She did not recognize them at first and blasted them in her best 'french.' "What the damn-hell you mean sneaking into my place!?"

The men were not really startled by her reception for they were familiar with her special personality. She had settled in the area as an early homesteader...always had been a loner...tough as nails. She could stand up to any man or beast and hold her own. The big gun she always had handy by her side helped. It was hard to live in this desolate country alone but Mrs. Halderman held the respect of everyone.

Seated at her counter as she served them, she, Don José and Frank chatted. They discussed the last rain – as everywhere among ranch people, the weather was always a favorite subject – and livestock.

"I'm missing a couple of cows, Don José. Wonder if any of your *vaqueros* have seen them?" Mrs. Halderman said.

Don José told her about what the cowboy had told Manuel. "I hope none of your cattle get into those weeds."

After a short while Don José and Frank excused themselves and continued on to Galisteo. It would be easy to stay and chat with neighbors along the route, but there was always too much work waiting for them at home.

For thirty years, Frank would drive his father back and forth from Galisteo to *Agua Verde* and would be at his side in all the moments of joy as well as the periods of sorrow.

Upon their return to Galisteo, there was a great deal of unfinished business and piles of new business to attend to.

"A letter of importance, Patrón! It appears to be from none other than the Governor," the clerk announced as he handed Don José his mail.

"He never relents in his endeavor to have me run for the Legislature," Don José sighed as he opened the letter. "Perhaps it is time for me to get it over with," he added with a twinkle in his eye.

And soon he would run and become a fine legislator. His feeling for people and, above all, his concern for their future kept him willing to serve in this very unappreciated profession. In those days, as today, politics only took from the man, never willing to really recognize what the man tried to accomplish. But Don José realized that New Mexico was changing and he wanted a part in the enactment of new laws. Land problems were beginning to crop up more frequently and fences could be seen in areas one would have thought were inaccessible and uninhabitable. There would be many laws passed that could hurt this land he loved so dearly but he would do his best to preserve its beauty.

The Patrón burning cactus during drought.

seven

It was a ritual with Don José and Frank to hold court in the store immediately after dinner each evening. Their workers and anyone else who wished to visit would drop by. In nice weather, they sat on a long wooden bench in front of the store. In inclement weather, they sat in the two chairs Don José carefully placed behind the old, woodstove opposite his office door. They would sit and visit, exchange news and listen to problems. The people would casually arrive and stay until the cantina closed; they knew the store would close shortly after. The cantina clerk would then meet with the store clerk and the two would balance the day's books. After this, Frank would review the ledgers and account for the daily receipts, and then the clerks called it a day. There were no eight hour days for any of the workers – or for Don José or Frank – but the store and cantina clerks had the longest hours, usually from seven in the morning until nine in the evening.

Many clerks came and went. One of the most colorful was Señor José Colón, whom everyone called Joe Columbus. He was a strange appearing man, not quite five feet tall and he had a hunch which protruded from his chest and back. Don José had found him in Canyon Blanco, a small settlement on the west boundary of *Agua Verde*. Joe had been highly recommended. People considered him a genius, and close to it he was. Joe was an avid reader, self-taught, and a whiz at mathematics. For years he served the Patrón and was trusted absolutely. But José Colón was a loner – perhaps because of his physical deformity – and was not well liked by the store customers. He remained businesslike and aloof. When he finally left Don José's employ, it was because various villagers had harassed him in an insulting manner.

"I feel it is time to move on, Patrón," he regretfully told Don José one day. The two parted with sadness. Don José felt he was losing a friend.

Another worker the Patrón held in great esteem and one popular with everyone was a man called Isabel Adams. He was half-Indian and an all around handyman. He chopped wood, tended to the fireplaces and stoves in the main buildings. A very quiet man, never a step away from the Patrón when he was at Galisteo.

There were many colorful and interesting people around Don José. He attracted people from every walk of life. He gave every man a chance, rarely turning any person away. And if he did not have a job for him, Don José created one.

One cold winter day, perhaps the finest *vaquero* the Patrón would ever have appeared. He was small, five feet in stature, dark complectioned with a contagious smile. As he entered the store, he walked over to the woodstove to warm his hands and asked for the Patrón. Don José was in the office and upon hearing the man's voice, asked Frank to show him in. "*Sí, Señor*. What can I do for you?" Don José asked.

"*Señor Don José*, I would like to be one of your *vaqueros*," the man replied.

With his practiced ability to judge men quickly, Don José returned the man's smile and said to Frank, "You'll have to find a small pony for this man to ride."

Entering the fun, Frank said, "What about a good-sized goat?"

"What is your name, my good friend?" Don José asked.

"My name is Reyes Montoya and you don't own or know of a horse that I cannot ride, Señor," Reyes declared.

"We are only joking, Reyes. But if I'm not mistaken, you are a man with a sense of humor. Anyway, a man will always prove himself and his words. I like your smile. Tomorrow, I will let you ride a horse all my *vaqueros* refuse to ride," Don José told him.

"I will ride him, Don José!" Reyes declared.

"Go and report to my *mayordomo*. He is in the bunkhouse. You will be fed and given a warm bed. Tomorrow we will watch you ride, Reyes. "*Gracias, Patrón!* I will see you in the morning," the happy Reyes replied.

The next morning after breakfast, Don José ordered a smoky bay named Día saddled for Reyes. He was a magnificent animal, sixteen hands, but rebellious – especially when saddled. None of the Patrón's *vaqueros* wanted to deal with Día.

"You can't trust him" one told Reyes.

Once the saddle was on, Don José called, "There he is Reyes. If you ride him and quiet him, you have a job. You also have a horse!"

All the hands had gathered to watch and they laughed, never believing this tiny man would stay on the horse. Reyes took the bridle and led Día away from the crowd. He led Día beside a corral gate and lowered his head so that his mouth could touch Día's ear. Reyes did not whisper in Día's ear, but bit it so hard the horse gave a mighty jerk, then – to the surprise of the onlookers – quickly calmed. Reyes hopped on the corral gate using it as a ladder and was off! Día made one full circle and stopped. He was Reyes' horse. The other *vaqueros* couldn't believe what they had seen.

"What did you do to that horse, Reyes?" Don José asked. He was very pleased with the performance.

"Nothing really, Patrón. I just told him I was boss. To prove it, I bit his ear. I have made many horses respect me this way," replied the new hand.

Reyes Montoya became one of Don José's most trusted and valued *vaqueros*. Never again did he have to prove his worth.

Frank went to Santa Fe every weekend to see Doña Pablita. On one weekend, his eyes fell on a beautiful and popular señorita from Santa Fe. The young lady was Maria Garcia, the daughter of Samuel and Josefita Garcia. She was the granddaughter of Samuel Ellison, a Kentuckian who had come to New Mexico during the Mexican War. He was a military man who later was associated with the courts in New Mexico. Samuel Ellison married Francisca Sanchez, so Maria was also the descendant of a fine family. At the time Frank met her she was living in Santa Fe and was the 'belle of the ball.' She was much admired and sought after and Frank was soon aware of his competition. But after a year of courtship – following all tradition and custom – the pair became engaged and set a date for their marriage.

Don José and Doña Pablita, in collaboration with the now-widowed Doña Josefita Garcia, planned and presented their children, Frank and Maria, with one of the most beautiful weddings ever held in St. Francis Cathedral. Upon their return from a brief honeymoon, Frank and Maria were given a home in Santa Fe by Don José, only a block away from Doña Pablita's. Frank and Maria decided she would reside in Santa Fe, for they wanted a large family and their children's education would have to be considered.

Frank returned to Galisteo with Don José and for years they would drive to Santa Fe twice weekly to be with their wives. Frank and Maria would have five children: Maria, José, Juan, Frank and Margaret. They would all be named Ortiz y Davis, except José who would be Ortiz y Pino in order to perpetuate that part of the family name.

He was the first son born to Frank and Maria and they chose to name him after Don José.

Depression clouds were now forming over the whole country. Soon the United States would be in the worst economic crisis in its history. The small Southwestern villages would feel it but families who worked for the Patrón would ride out the Depression without too many scars. This period in New Mexico history held enormous promise for those who continued to strive for their dreams. Many would fall by the wayside, but land and livestock owners would be able to weather the ensuing crises because they were willing to sacrifice. Don José, with his compassionate philosophy and his faith in God, would stand fast throughout the Depression and would become much stronger.

Another Spring! There was too much to do to be fully aware that many people were out of work or that strangers by the hundreds were descending on the village of Galisteo looking for work or a meal. All these people were not allowed to go hungry for the villagers would send them to Don José and, of course, their needs were met.

Lambing season approached and Don José would hire many of these strangers to help him deliver his lambs.

Don José had more time to devote to his personal feelings now that Frank was taking more and more responsibility. Don José found himself more than once with tears in his eyes, especially in the early morning hours as he observed the celestial bodies. "God! I stand before You so insignificant, such a small part of Your creation, and yet You give me so much, especially my son, who is virtually a replica of me. Thank You,

Lord, for I now realize that contentment is not the fulfillment of what you want, but the realization of how much you already have." He would pray to his God and thank Him. With this faith, he was ready to go on.

"Frank, tomorrow we leave for *Agua Verde*. Is everything prepared for lambing," he asked his son.

"Yes, but I pray for one thing. The beautiful May showers, for it has been such a dry winter," Frank answered. This was always the hope and prayer of sheep owners...good rains so the flocks would have fresh, rich, young grass to pass on to their newborn lambs in the form of rich and strong milk.

A great many of the preparations took place at the Galisteo hacienda. Supplies and feed had to be delivered on a daily basis to *Agua Verde*. Men were assigned specific jobs and *veladores* (night watchmen) were designated. Some men were selected to be with *atajos* (small groups of newborn lambs) and yet others would have chores around the *ahijatero* (lambing quarters). Then, of course, there were the cooks and their helpers. Preparation was undertaken much like a military operation. Men were sent along daily with the supplies and when all was ready, the Patrón and Frank would go to *Agua Verde* and closely supervise the birth of thousands of lambs.

Don José and Frank stayed at the rock home which had been built for them at Melás. It would be home for them for at least two weeks or until the majority of the lambs were born. Rams were bred to the ewes only during a certain period in the fall so that lambing would occur during a certain spring month. Ewes the rams did not breed were later used for food or were sold.

Four lambing stations were established. Each station would operate identically to the other and the Patrón made certain that the most experienced *mayordomo* supervised the operation. Huge herds of sheep would encircle the lambing area and as ewes were ready to give birth, they were separated. If the weather was cold or stormy, they would be placed under sheds at night. A night watchman would see that all went well during the night hours. As the ewes gave birth, they were turned out with their babies in small groups so the herders could watch to be sure each baby lamb was nursing and that all the ewes were accepting their own lambs. The work went on twenty-four hours a day and the most popular man had to be the *cocinero* (cook). He had huge pots of coffee and mountains of food ready at all times for the men who were working around the clock. It was also a fun time. Men would exchange stories and news between work shifts. There was always time for jokes and the young herders were usually the butt of most of them.

The Patrón and Frank would make the rounds of the different stations and keep a tally-book as to the numbers of lambs being born. They would check the supplies and make certain they kept flowing in from Galisteo. They always gave praise and, of course, criticism when necessary to the men. The Patrón demanded they handle their jobs well. He demanded a keen eye and honest answers from these workers who looked after his sheep. The lambs were small creatures of God and could not fend for themselves very well for the first few days. There was always the danger of coyotes and eagles. On one occasion, a pack of coyotes hit a small bunch of ewes and lambs. When the coyotes had finished, there were thirty or more dead lambs. The herders faced many perils of this kind.

After a hearty dinner of *costillar de borrega* (lamb ribs), *frijoles*, *papas fritas*, (fried peasant potatoes), topped off with a plate of *melás* (molasses syrup) which was sopped off the plate with a warm piece of homemade bread, the Patrón and his men would retire to one of the bunkhouses and, sitting by the fire, would exchange news and stories.

This particular evening, one of the men brought up the story of a love he found but quickly lost. "Patrón, do you remember Dolores Flores who lived at the Lopez settlement?" he asked.

"Yes, Antonio. What has happened to her? She has not come to the door to greet me the last few times I have been there to see Señor Flores," Don José replied.

"Well, I met her one day when I went to resupply and we had a hurried but good visit. After that, everytime I went there for supplies we would manage to sneak a few moments together. We started to make serious plans but one day when I went to see her she explained we must not see each other again. I asked her why but she would not tell me. So, I left with my heart in deep pain. I went back a month ago and inquired about Dolores and was told she was living at *Guajalotes* with Señor Martin Ortega. I could not believe it and continued to inquire. My informant related the events that had taken place. Señor Ortega had homesteaded on the south boundary of *Agua Verde* and had become quite wealthy as his flock of sheep grew. About the time he took Dolores with him, he was in his late sixties and Dolores was barely fifteen. Señor Ortega had made a deal with Señor Flores, Dolores' father, to give him a ten acre tract of land where he could plant beans in exchange for Dolores who would be given in marriage to Señor Ortega. The girl had no choice. She had many brothers and sisters and she was the eldest. Her father wanted the land so he, too, could be a landowner. Dolores did not love Señor Ortega but her father will not discuss the subject other than to tell people who inquire that it was of her own free will," Antonio told them.

"Why have you waited so long to tell me this, Antonio?" Don José asked. "This is not like Señor Flores. I will speak to him tomorrow. He is at the La Madera lambing station."

"Patrón, I thought maybe someone else had told you. I love Dolores but I don't think much can be done now," Antonio said sadly.

"I think you are right, Antonio. But he will not work or live on my property. He must go and make his living from the ten acres with his bean plants. His children and his wife can work for me anytime. I will tell him tomorrow that he must comply with his part of the deal! Don José said.

The other men listening to the story agreed with their Patrón. So it was, the next morning the Patrón and Frank visited La Madera lambing station. Lambing was going well: one hundred new babies had been born that night. Rosendo Garcia, the *mayordomo* at that station, greeted his Patrón and *Patrón chiquito* (the little patrón), as the men were starting to call Frank. After greetings were exchanged and new tallies were entered in the Patrón's book, Rosendo commented he had been doing as the Patrón had ordered with young lambs that were born dead. He was taking their pelts and placing them on the backs of orphaned lambs. The mother with a dead lamb would think that the orphan was hers because of the scent and would accept the orphan lamb as hers. It was a good idea and it gave many a young lamb a chance for a new mother. After a few weeks, the dead lamb's pelt was removed from the orphan's back and the mother never knew the difference.

Don José asked for Señor Flores and was told that he was up at the house. When Don José arrived Señor Flores came out to greet him. Don José greeted him cordially, then confronted him with the story he had heard.

"Patrón, it is true," Señor Flores admitted.

"Well, then you will comply with my wishes," Don José told him and proceeded to advise him that he would have to leave his property. Señor Flores realized justice was being meted out. Whether it was his personal business or not, whatever happened on the Patrón's land was the Patrón's business. Don José could not tolerate the exchanging of a human being for a piece of land. He was not God, but he would ask for respect and demand honesty from all who worked or lived on his land.

Señor Flores complied with the mandate. Soon after he moved to his bean patch, new people came to live at La Madera. Many incidents such as this would take place during the Patrón's life. As the Patrón, people expected he would always be fair and just when problems of all kinds came before him.

Once lambing was over, the stations were disbanded and the best *pastores* were given large herds of ewes and lambs to care for until shearing time when once again all the herds would be gathered to continue with another phase of the sheep raising business.

Galisteo house ruins after World War II.

Black karakul lamb.

eight

The Patrón and Frank returned to Galisteo and tried to rest a few days before continuing their arduous tasks of ranching. But during this period Don Pedro, the Patrón's brother, passed away and Don José went through a time of profound sadness. God had been good to Don Pedro and he had hard-working children who would continue for a time in the sheep business as Don Pedro had done most of his life.

The Galisteo ranches were slowly being changed from sheep to cattle. This wide-open land in the Galisteo Basin, with less rainfall than the *Agua Verde* properties, was better suited for the far-ranging cow. The sheep would dig up what grass they did not eat with their cloven hooves. The cow was not quite so destructive.

During the Depression, livestock was a liability to those people who did not have sufficient land for their herds to run on and, at the same time, the area was experiencing a severe drought. The Federal Government (in its most charitable manner!) began offering stockraisers five dollars for every cow they would kill and many had to stand by and watch this done to their herds. After the slaughter, the beef was offered to the people.

The Patrón believed that when these bad times passed, there would be a demand for cattle and sheep once again. In preparation, he and Frank started to implement the *partido* system: they would give ten cows to a landowner, wherever he might be, and would charge him one-half of his calf crop each year. The plan was well received by many people, especially when the rains began again. People who had killed off their livestock could replace their herds in time. This partido system would enable Don José to provide more cattle for the Galisteo area and also increase the herds at *Agua Verde*. He would often comment, "Not once have I lost on a partido contract." And the people with whom he dealt almost always achieved a new start for themselves.

Except for the time spent in Santa Fe with their families, Don José and Frank were always busy with the now-huge empire they had created. Don José continued his life of physical activity and as challenges presented themselves, he was always fit and eager to pursue them. Don José always maintained his appearance. He was a very dignified figure: dressing daily in a suit, vest and tie he was ready for any occasion. In contrast, Frank would dress a little more like the ranch workers, but would still present an appearance of authority.

One evening while they were sitting in their chairs at the store and a few people had gathered to talk with them, Frank asked his father to relate the saga of Doña Tules.

"My son, why are you interested in Doña Tules? What on earth made you come up with that subject?" Don José asked.

"I've heard a lot of stories about her being related to us, Papa. I've also heard that with her gambling casinos and bordelos, she actually ran the State. Is this true?" Frank replied.

Don José laughed. "Frank, I never knew the lady called La Tules (Lady of the River Reeds), but, yes, she was a relative. She almost got your great-grandfather, Nicholás Pino, into jail. Her time of life was during the 1820s and ended in 1852, when death claimed her. Doña Tules died very young. She was only in her thirties. So, I can only re-count to you what you grandfather told me about her, and he, of course, was told about her by Don Nicholás," Don José said.

"Go ahead, Papa. Tell me all you can remember," Frank said eagerly.

Don José continued. "She was born in the Golden area and when about ten years old she moved with her family to Santa Fe. When she was fourteen, she started to clean house for one of the *Capitanes* of the Mexican Occupation Forces. During the time she was serving as a house cleaner, the Capitán became attracted to her. She was supposed to be a very beautiful young lady. Events followed events and he seduced her. As a reward for his conquest, he presented her with a five peso gold piece. Your great-grandfather said she looked at the gold piece and commented, 'What would a General give me?'

"Presently, she became the favorite of other officers and men in high office. She was diligent and saved her earnings. In time, she invested in a building off the Plaza in Santa Fe and opened a casino-bordello com-bination. Doña Tules was on her way! The story was told she would select the men with whom she played cards. She would keep them waiting until late in the evening and then make her grand entrance. Doña Tules did all the things women were not allowed to do in those times, including smoking in public. As the evening progressed and she sat playing with the men she selected, it became very evident she was winning and her opponents did not seem to mind at all. The reason was that she had a set policy: the man who lost the most would have the privilege of taking her upstairs to her room after the casino closed for the night.

"People would often tease your great-grandfather, Nicholás Pino, 'You've lost more money to her than to any man!' One thing he almost lost because of her was his freedom. Don Nicholás Pino and a group of men from Santa Fe were plotting to overthrow the Mexican Governor in Santa Fe. Doña Tules was having an affair with the Governor and to further her ambitions of power, she revealed the plot to the Governor. He ordered the arrest of the plotters but they fled Santa Fe before they could be arrested. Your great-grandfather never forgave Doña Tules for that.

"Doña Tules controlled the political life of New Mexico because she 'had the goods' on every official in Santa Fe. She and her business prospered and before long she was expanding into the Taos area. Doña Tules also ventured out into the rural settlements and many times she 'set up business' at your grandmother's hacienda across the street.

"At this time, the Vicar General in Santa Fe became very concerned with Doña Tules. He felt her activities were corrupting the morals of Santa Fe. He was not the only one who was ready to castigate Doña Tules for her activities. Her family was turning against her. The Vicar General felt he must put a stop to her open contempt for Christian morals. The Vicar – equivalent to a Bishop – sent her a message by one of his friars advising her if she did not change her ways he would make sure she would not receive a Christian burial or the Sacraments on her death. He also advised her she would be excommunicated if she failed to heed his warning. Doña Tules received the message and advised the friar she hated to disagree with His Excellency but all these threats would only amount to threats and that she could safely predict her funeral would be the grandest ever in Santa Fe.

"Her many family members who also were willing to disown her were scoffed at by Doña Tules and she continued with her life. A few years before her death, she married a man named Barcelo. He patiently accepted her life style. At the moment of her death, at her instructions, Barcelo was supposed to deliver separate messages in sealed envelopes to the Vicar General and to all those members of her family who held her in such great contempt. Barcelo carried out her will after she took her last breath."

Isabel Adams, the loyal keeper of the fires, interrupted Don José. "Patrón, your bedroom is ready. The stove is really going good." The story was of no importance to Isabel, but his Patrón's comfort was.

"Fine, Isabel. But, sit down and let me finish this story. I had almost forgotten that it was getting so late," Don José said and continued. "Anyway, the notes were delivered and the results were unbelievable. Doña Tules had the finest Funeral Mass and funeral that Santa Fe had not seen the likes of for a long time and the Vicar General was also present. Her family members cried and cried and expounded on their love for her. Later it would become known that in the message to the Vicar General she demanded this fine funeral and as a reward he would receive five thousand gold pieces. Each member of her family would receive five hundred gold pieces if they would cry from the moment of her death 'til the moment the last shovelfull of dirt was placed on her remains. You see, Frank, she had her way. You can believe this story or not, but I've told it to you as it was related to me." Don José smiled as he finished.

"Thank you, Papa! How fantastic her power reached back from the grave," Frank exclaimed. "I had heard many stories of this lady, and how she ran the government from her casinos, but I did not realize how Don Nicholás Pino had been involved."

"Let's go to sleep, son. Isabel wants to get some sleep also," Don José said and rose to go to bed. Isabel would also sleep in the room next to Don José and Frank for he would have to keep the fires stoked throughout the night. It was also Isabel's task to handle the many strangers who knocked at Don José's door during the night. Isabel was a good and faithful worker.

Summer came again and shearing season was upon them. The Patrón prepared as extensively for the shearing of his sheep as he did for their lambing. Once he and Frank arrived at *Agua Verde*, the process would begin at every station. The herds of sheep would be driven into an area surrounding the station and wait their turn. All the shearing was originally done by hand with shears very similar to a large pair of scissors. Men were designated for this job on the basis of experience and patience. It was perhaps one of the most tedious and time consuming occupations in the sheep business.

As the first herd was penned in the corrals, the sheep were separated into smaller pens where the shearers had a tent set up for shade. At the end of this pen was a platform where the sacks were filled with the wool as it was shorn from the sheep. Each shearer had his own method but usually he would select the sheep by feeling its wool and in this way would get all the easy ones first. The sheep without too much dirt and with good, long wool were the fastest to clip. The shearers were paid by the head and some of the best could shear sixty sheep a day.

During these years, wool shearers were coming in from South Texas. It was they who introduced the first shearing machines to New Mexico. With these gas-operated machines a man could easily do more than a hundred sheep a day. The shearing crews set up their camps a little distance from the lambing stations. The South Texans were usually Mexicans and stayed more to themselves. They worked very hard and by the time the sun went down they were ready to eat and sleep. The Patrón and Frank would sometimes walk over to their camp and visit with the *mayordomo* of the shearing camp. They enjoyed listening to the tales of the South Texas country and how life was across the border. It also gave Don José and Frank an opportunity to study the language which was a little different than the Spanish spoken in New Mexico. The Patrón never for a moment forgot his belief that there was always much to learn from people if you were willing to listen.

Shearing usually lasted at least two weeks and when the shearers finished with the *Agua Verde* herds, they would travel to Galisteo and shear the sheep the Patrón had there. The wool was stacked in huge piles. Each burlap sack held at least five hundred pounds. Before the advent of trucks, Don José would have them hauled from *Agua Verde* to the warehouse in Galisteo by wagon which involved a considerable number of wagons with many days of breakdowns and other problems on the cross country road to Galisteo. Tarps covered the precious wool since the least bit of moisture could ruin it. Once the wool arrived at the wool warehouse, the men would unload it and stack it as neatly as they could. There it would await shipment to the Boston markets.

The shearing season was another opportunity for the Patrón to visit with all his men on a daily basis. The families from the settlements would bring the small children to witness this interesting event, and of course the young ladies would look forward to displaying their 'wares' to all the unmarried men they knew gathered at the shearing stations. Don José enjoyed visiting with the small children and encouraged them to attend the rural schools. He would advise them and make them feel important. In his heart he realized that they needed more encouragement than the children in the larger towns. But the base of all his advice was that they honor their parents and remember that only hard work would pay rewards. All the children respected the Patrón and were in awe of him for he symbolized success and power – but more importantly, love. The families working for Don José felt that in their moments of strife and need they could always come to Don José and would receive action about their problems rather than only words. It was not a easy life to be a Patrón but as Don José thought back to the time of Don Juan, he could now realize the responsibilities which went with the title.

After the shearing was completed, some *pastores* would get time off and others, who had not been with the herds as long, would assume their duties till they returned from *remuda*. The single *pastores* would head for the closest town or their own village and for thirty days would 'live it up,' drinking and chasing the young ladies. The older married men returned to their wives and families and, with their earnings, buy their families all the things they dreamed of – shoes, dresses, a phonograph and so on. This buying spree would go on until everything was spent. During their time off, the men would talk of not returning to work for the Patrón, that perhaps things were better somewhere else. They would go in search, but before long they were at the Patrón's door. He always welcomed them and would set a date for them to report for work and at the same time advance them at least a month's salary. The cycle would repeat itself during the year. They would probably work nine months and be off three.

The young men spent their money much faster than the older *pastores*. The ones who lived in Galisteo would either leave their money at the Patrón's cantina or find a way to Santa Fe. Once in Santa Fe, there were some favorite haunts with names like *La Mariposa*, The Butterfly, and *El Cid*. At these famous bars, short work was made of their wages by either the bartenders or the lovely ladies of the night. These famous ladies were given nicknames by their clients. Some of the more interesting names were *La Mula*, the mule, *La Take It Easy*, *La Yequa*, the mare and *La Chispa*, the spark. When the men returned from their adventures, they knew there would be a lot of time to compare notes by the light of their campfires.

Respect and courtesy were important in these people's lives. There was no time for racial prejudice. The closest they ever came to negative prejudice was when a negro would come traveling through the country. The people did not look down at him, but they did regard him as an unfortunate creature of God who was born the wrong color. The *gringo* was admired, not hated as so many people thought. The Patrón would always emphasize to his people, "Study the *gringo*, for he will give you new ideas."

As always, the summer went by much too fast and the rains had turned the countryside into beautiful fields of black grama grass and large-stemmed salt grass. Even the small ring grasses would abound when the land was blessed by rain. The pace of life in Galisteo remained unchanged. A number of people had left during the Depression but those who had stayed were feeling the winds of change. Don José was still the center of life in Galisteo. Age was not stopping the Patrón. During the thirties, Don José was in his fifties, but his strict physical and mental regime kept him in marvelous condition. Accompanied by Frank, Don José would visit his Galisteo ranches every day he could. Once at his destination, he would take off, cane in hand, and walk for an hour or two to see the land and his animals from their level. As they would walk along, he would tell his son, "Frank, this land is not really ours. We are simply caretakers. Our purpose in this life is to be good to the land and try to leave it better than we found it!"

"Papa, that seems impossible. When our forefathers came into this part of the country, this was all wilderness. Only the Indians trekked across it. We have put sheep and cattle on it. Some areas have suffered by overgrazing. How do we leave it better?" Frank asked.

"But think, son, what we have done for these lands! We stop erosion wherever we see it. We try not to overgraze. We fence it into smaller areas where we can control it better. We have people living on it and raising fine children. Our intentions and actions are sincere. We cannot stop the change of this land by man and his ambition, but we can make sure that it is done in an orderly manner."

"Yes, I see what you mean and I realize some 'caretakers' are better than others," Frank answered.

"In future generations, my son, land will be as valuable and as scarce as diamonds," Don José added.

Don José was never afraid to try something new. One day upon awakening he commented to Frank, "Son, why don't we plant winter wheat in all these flat pieces of land we have around the village? We'll need certain equipment to prepare the soil and to plant the wheat, but I am sure we can order it."

And so winter wheat was planted and whenever there was good winter moisture the early spring would bring beautiful green fields to the south of Galisteo. Every crop was important and with care and patience there was so much to reap in this beautiful land. At *La Jara* (the willow) Ranch, which was south of the village, there were a number of long draws which, in the summer provided it rained, produced large quantities of grass. The Patrón would send mowing machines drawn by large mules to cut it. The grass was then piled up and hauled to the headquarters where it would provide good winter feed for the animals kept there.

On more than one occasion, while the men were cutting the grass, the mowers would slice into a den of rattlesnakes. This was always dangerous for the men following the mower. The snakes, angered and bewildered, would strike out at the first thing that moved. One of the Patrón's most trusted workers was bitten in the face. His face and head swelled to the size of a pumpkin. He was taken immediately to Doña

Josefita at Galisteo. This was a difficult job for her as the fang marks were on the man's upper lip. With her experience and knowledge, she ordered one of the girls to prepare a mixture of wild *osha* (parsley family) and *calabazilla* (squash family) in a vat. When it had boiled, Doña Josefita gave him a cup of the brew to drink and washed his face and neck in the solution. She could not bleed him very well where the fang marks were, but she made a small incision in one of his neck veins and detoured the blood with poison in that manner. Then she sent the man to remain quiet and rest in bed. In a few days he was as good as new.

Doña Josefita Davis was quickly losing her eyesight. She was frail with age and would be leaving this earth soon. The Patrón knew that this fine woman would be greatly missed. She had become an historical part of the village.

Branding time was in the air! Each event came fast on the heels of the last and there was no time to stop and rest. To maintain his empire, it was essential when one event ended the Patrón was planning the next.

The cattle at *Agua Verde* would be gathered first and when branding was finished there, the Galisteo cattle would be next. It was important to try to work the cattle after a rain and before the weather became hot, for freshly branded and castrated calves were easy prey to flies and worms.

A date was set. The cattle would be driven to the Melás settlement where the Patrón had built large and efficient corrals. It would take Don José's *vaqueros* at least a week to gather the cattle that roamed on his land and still the cowboys would never get some of them rounded up.

Extra cooking facilites and sleeping tents were set up. Supplies were brought in from Galisteo daily so when the day the gathered herd was driven to the branding corrals, everything was ready.

The herd was penned in these huge corrals and the calves were separated from their mothers. The over-zealous bulls were also penned separately. The men selected to tend the huge piñon fire used to heat the branding irons would start the fire early that morning. The hotter the iron, the faster it would burn the brand on the young calves. Don José would supervise the whole operation and Frank would do all the castrating with the help of Manuel.

As the calves were roped and dropped by the *vaqueros,* men would hold the front and back legs, making certain the calves could not kick loose. Frank then cut the testicles out in a very surgical and rapid manner. In his many years of doing this, he seldom lost a calf. He would place the testicles in a bucket used only for that purpose and when the *vaqueros* stopped for lunch, the men tending the fires would place the testicles on the piñon coals to cook. All the men looked forward to this tasteful treat. Visitors would be coaxed to try this delicacy while the *vaqueros* laughed at their doubtful expressions.

The calves were branded with the J.O. Bar brand, checked and released. Branding went on all day and usually by sunset the herd that had been brought in would be finished. That herd would be released the following morning and the remaining cattle and calves were branded whenever they were found. Some were never found for rustling was always a factor in this country. It was not people who needed the meat to eat who did the rustling but rather groups of men who would drive the cattle to concealed areas and then either change the brands or brand unbranded cattle with their brand. Most of these stolen cattle were driven to ranches far away from *Agua Verde* and either sold or butchered.

There was one family of rustlers who operated out of the Las Vegas area. The Patrón suspected they had been making lucrative business with his cattle, so he set a trap to catch these men.

Don José's *vaqueros* determined that a box canyon on the south side of the ranch was the place the rustlers used. They would drive as many cattle as they could into the box canyon and leave them there for a day or two. When the Patrón's *vaqueros* went by the box canyon they would see the cattle grazing peacefully and suspect nothing. Then a day later, the rustlers, knowing the *vaqueros* had seen the cattle undisturbed, would come and drive them over the ridge to the corrals of one of the neighbor's. Don José instructed his *vaqueros* to inform the *mayordomo* when they saw his cattle in the box canyon and he would place *vaqueros* on the rim of the canyon at strategic spots.

The Patrón's plan was carried out. The rustlers came in late one afternoon and started gathering the cattle. As soon as they had finished, Don José's *vaqueros* rode down from the sides of the canyon toward the men and joined them.

"Where are you going with this herd, my friends?" Don José's *mayordomo* inquired.

The rustlers were scared to death, but one of them – the leader – answerd, "Oh, we were just going to drive them over that ridge and direct them toward Melás. We were afraid they would wander away from here!"

"That's very nice of you, but Don José told us you might be trying to steal them and if that was the case, he ordered us to castrate every one of you," the *mayordomo* told them.

"No! No! Friend, we would not steal from Don José. Please! We will never come around here again," the leader pleaded.

"You are lucky, then. I know every one of you and if we are ever short one cow, the Patrón will send us for you," the *mayordomo* told them before he left.

Don José never had to send for them. They had been caught and knew better than to gamble on a second time.

Don José's manner of dealing out justice to those who injured him or his possessions was compassionate. He never would have physically harmed the cattle rustlers or turned them in to the authorities unless the persisted in their actions. In another instance when some of his men robbed the wool warehouse in Galisteo, he was forced to report it to the authorities for some of the wool belonged to other sheep raisers. At the end of that episode after the men were convicted of their crime, he used his political influence to get the men out on probation. His feelings were that, as human beings, we are all tempted at least once in our lifetimes to follow bad advice or to make a bad decision. His compassionate views for his people served to endear him even more to the people who called him Patrón. Whenever there were land disputes or when their children ran into problems with the law, the Patrón was there. Don José's political influence gave him great leverage in helping people deal with the problems that government sometimes created. Many in this area could not read or write and there was always a stack of requests on his desk for him to read a letter, make out a deed or a will – an assortment which he or Frank always obliged.

Don José's office soon became a place for people in high office to visit. On more than one occasion, you would find candidates for U.S. Senator, Governor and the like, visiting him. His help was sought for two main reasons: First, a lot of people worked for him and the politicians felt that Don José could influence votes in their favor. Secondly, Don José would always give them a monetary contribution. He would remind them at a later date of his contributions, especially if they won.

For a period in the late thirties, Don José was offered the nomination for Governor. The office was his for the taking as the convention was controlled by his friends. But he turned the offer down. He was not to be the king, but rather, the king-maker. The men who did become Governors appointed him to board positions over a period of years. He was on the State Prison and the State Police Boards, then the Highway Board. The latter he enjoyed, for he was able to build beautiful bridges around Galisteo and good highways wherever they were needed on a bigger scale than when he was a County Commissioner.

World War II was on the agenda, and more changes would come to Galisteo. The Patrón would feel some of them deeply.

At this time, Doña Josefita Davis passed away at a grand old age, and with her passing, another era was coming to an end. She gave substance to the old beliefs and traditions. Life would never be the same without the woman who had been so many things to so many people. Doña Pablita and José acquired the old hacienda which later would be given to their son, Frank.

The Patrón feeding cattle.

nine

With the onset of World War II people started leaving the area. Most went to California to work at aircraft plants but others would travel north to the big industrial cities such as Detroit and Chicago. Young men were being called into the service, some of whom the Patrón could have deferred since his business was essential to the War effort. Frank was deferred to help his father. Don José's empire was at its peak now and help was not easy to acquire. All he had wanted and worked for had been accomplished. He delegated more and more of the work load to Frank. These were hard years for him, even more difficult than the Depression. The older men who had been with Don José since they were children were now the main work force. Food and gas rationing created difficulties but could not equal the change that was in the air. The people who remained tried to continue their normal pace of life but each time word came from the War Department that a son or friend had been killed, the War came closer to Galisteo.

Religious services and special masses kept the parish priest extra busy and the people did not lose faith. Religious feasts retained their color. On Christmas Eve one could see *luminarias* (stacks of piñon firewood) burning in front of the church and many of the homes had the traditional *farolitos* (paper bags with lighted candles) burning warmly at their entrances. Midnight Mass, or *La Misa del Gallo* (Mass of the rooster), was still observed and afterward the people would scatter to different homes to partake of large bowls of *posole* (treated hominy stewed with chili and pork skins). Early on Christmas morning, the young children would parade from house to house with a borrowed stocking which they hoped would be filled with candies and cookies. Later on Christmas Day *Las Posadas* was presented. This was a theatrical presentation depicting Joseph and Mary searching for shelter at Bethlehem, carried out year after year by a group of people. The actors would weave their way through the village going from house to house, knocking at the doors, asking for a place for the night. The Blessed Mother Mary was portrayed by a young, virgin girl selected by members of the cast. She rode on a burro led by St. Joseph in the procession. According to tradition, all the homes except one would turn the Holy Family away. The home selected to offer a place for Mary's Child to be born would bestow gifts of money and food on the Christ Child. The costumes and painted faces were a marvel to witness. Many of the actors vied to out-do each other in their creations. The old Spanish dialogue and the songs were soul-stirring.

Don José and Frank always enjoyed these celebrations and did all they could to insure their success. For these ancient customs were a part of their religious culture and Frank and Don José felt they needed to be continued and taught to future generations.

World War II was taking its toll on Don José. Workers were more and more difficult to find so the Patrón began to cut the size of his herds. He sold all the sheep from the Galisteo area and kept only his cattle. In *Agua Verde*, he cut his herds in half. To make matters worse, a great drought which lasted six years set in.

Sitting in the sun one beautiful spring day, Don José finally found himself admitting that time was running out for him. He searched deep within himself and all that would come was satisfaction. He was more than gratified with the success his God had bestowed on him. Don José was now in his middle sixties. He had noticed for some time that at moments his hands and legs trembled uncontrollably. Now it was happening more often. Frank was aware of these tremors which his father tried to hide but he would not discuss the matter until Don José wished to discuss it. As Don José sat there in the sun that day under the old pear tree which grew beside his office, his thoughts carried him back to his father, Don Juan. He always spoke quietly to his father but today he spoke somewhat louder. He wanted to be heard as he inquired of his dead father, "Papa Juan, have I pleased you? Am I now ready to join you?" He listened for an answer and not hearing one, he started to look back on his life. He scrutinized those things he felt he could have done better as well as those things that perhaps he should not have done at all.

Frank was in the office working as usual with the complete devotion he gave his growing obligations. He stepped out the door for a moment to catch a breath of fresh air and, seeing his father so peaceful and deep in thought, hesitated to bother him. Don José saw him out of the corner of his eye and asked Frank to join him.

"Frank, we always have so many things to talk about and I know we talk business all day long – sometimes late into the night. But, I want to visit with you – about us! About you and me and the future!" he said.

Frank sat beside his father in the warm sunshine.

Don José continued. "Frank, you are my only son and I have tried to prepare you to be a good Patrón. We have been blessed by God, and He has bestowed great landholdings and large herds of livestock on us. Our health has been good up to this point, but you have noticed the tremors of my hands and legs as well as other changes that are beginning to slow me down. You are practically running the entire business – and a fine job you are doing. Now, I must pass on all responsibility to you ...it is time for me to rest."

"Papa, you must not worry, for I can handle the work."

"Frank, I am grateful for your respect. We have many things to do in order to tie up loose ends so that when I no longer am here things will go smoothly. I have lands I want to be yours and others for your sisters. And, of course, your mother must come first. All these things we must do. We must go over all of my possessions and leave things in order. Long-time workers and people who need deeds for land that we have agreed to give them must be taken care of."

And so the Patrón and his son discussed the subjects they both had hoped they never would have to discuss.

"It was good," Don José thought as Frank returned to the office. "We have a course set. He understands what must be done. I have much to do, also. I will not stop till these infernal tremors put me in a bed."

That he did with all his power. He continued to help Frank and to be the Patrón.

World War II was over. The young men returning home did not feel they wanted to be *vaqueros* or *pastores* They had seen big cities and all the new and exciting creations a country at war could produce. They felt there was no future in Galisteo. Again there were great changes and they could sense them. Homes were abandoned and more people left

Galisteo and the villages. The people had heard about and seen President Roosevelt's New Deal with its professed opportunities, more wages and welfare programs. Why should they work as hard as their forefathers had? There was a great, new world out there. The Patrón System was not the answer anymore. Sure, some of them said, it was good for our fathers and mothers, and it helped us grow into men and women, but we cannot stay working for pennies. We must make our fortune somewhere else.

Frank would take the Patrón to *Agua Verde* at least once a week and the Patrón would survey his domain. He would remind Frank of all the families who once lived there in the now-abandoned homes in some of the settlements. He wondered if all was well with those who had left and asked if there was news from them.

Only a few families were still with the Patrón. Among the largest was Manuel's at Melás. Many of Manuel's children remained as *caporales*, overlooking the remaining herds of sheep and cattle. Under them, everything went on the same way – lambing, shearing, branding – but the events were not as large. Althought many changes could be seen, tradition remained strong and business went on as usual.

The Patrón would have Frank take him all over the ranch until he became tired. Then they would stop at a sheep camp and rest. This was his life. No matter how much power and wealth were his, he could fully feel his accomplishments and mission on earth in these remote and simple sheep camps. The coffee boiling over from the black and battered pot, spilling on the hot piñon coals, the aroma combining with the fresh air in this open country made him feel his closeness to the earth. The earth was his life. It had been good to him and his people. Sometimes it had caused tears and bitterness, especially when the droughts came. But with the first rains or snows, it seemed to make you forget the bad and give you courage to go forward. Yes, the land and all its plants and creatures could well attest to the Great Plan God was willing to share with His caretakers. The dependence of man on God's plants and animals and, in turn, their independence of man was powerfully demonstrated here around the shepherd's campfire.

"Everything we overlook so often all of a sudden becomes more important," Don José thought as he viewed the great thunderhead building up to the east. "Soon the rains will come again, and the parched earth will be born again and again. And so it will be with all the things that really matter on earth."

He could still remember the words of an old *pastor* he had employed when he started his first sheep herd. His name was Meliton. The old man always seemed to walk in a reckless manner, looking here and there, up and down, all the while taking deep breaths of air, whether it was a cold or warm day. Don José asked him one day, "Meliton, you are such a busy man. You are continually trying to see in every direction and also wanting to hurry so. Why is this?"

"Don José," the man answered, "don't you know all the best things in the world are free? They are yours for the taking. The air, the views, the stars and plants..." On and on he went until Don José stopped him.

"Is that why you try to take everything in, Meliton?" Don José asked.

"Yes, Patrón. Because soon I will be a rich man after I have seen all these things and they are then mine!"

Don José never forgot Meliton and told the story often to others.

On their drive back to Galisteo, the usual stops were made, including the one at Mrs. Halderman's. While the Patrón sipped his refreshment, Mrs. Halderman would bring him up on all the latest happenings in the area. Many of Don José's people stopped to visit with her as well as people from more distant ranches. She was kept well informed on what was going on. It was more a pleasure to hear her talk in her raspy, hurried way than actually hearing the news.

After they left her, they stopped at White Lakes, a small out-of-the-way service station and cafe. Years ago a lumber mill had been set up here to work lumber cut from the Patrón's land. The area was also a supply station which the Patrón used during severe winters. One year the snow came the first of December and kept falling, it seemed, through February! The snow grew to five feet on *Agua Verde* and campers and *vaqueros* would drive thirty or forty burros to White Lakes. There, they would be packed with supplies brought from Galisteo. Then they would trudge twelve to fifteen miles, criss-crossing *Agua Verde*, resupplying the settlements and camps. The Patrón referred to this area as "burro station." His memories of those winters were not his fondest.

After visiting with the kind people at White Lakes, they resumed their trip back to Galisteo. Don José said on the way, "The sun is still high. Let's stop and visit Benito Vigil. We haven't seen the *negras* (black ones) in a few days."

"Fine, Papa!" Frank smiled. "They seem to be your favorites."

Don José called the Karakul sheep which he introduced into this area *las negras*. They were from Russia, a long-haired breed of sheep that were usually black. The Patrón, never afraid to try something new, imported a herd of thirty. Now that herd numbered over five hundred. He read that new born lambs were killed moments after leaving the mothers' wombs, and that the skins were used to make coats which were called "broadtail" or "Persian lamb." He was quite successful selling the skins for a few years. During that time he also had made some beautiful coats and capes for the women in the family. But the market for the skins dropped and so the Patrón, instead, raised the sheep for the fine mohair they produced. Frank would kid him and say, "Papa, you couldn't stand killing those lambs before they took their first breath. That's why you no longer sell pelts." Don José would laugh but deep inside, he knew Frank was right.

As they located the herd of *negras* in the *piedra lumbre* (fire rock) pasture, which was just a few miles to the north of Galisteo, they saw Benito approaching with his dog. Benito was a great sight to behold. He had jet-black hair and possessed a fine handlebar moustache. He dressed in leather clothes which he fashioned himself from deer and goat skins. A sheep pelt hat adorned his head. Benito carried a long, rawhide whip in one hand and his cane in the other.

"Benito! How is our good friend today?" Don José called.

"I was all right, Patrón, until I saw you and the Little Patrón coming. Now, my day is ruined!" Benito laughed and cursed his luck.

"Well, Benito! Papa likes to come and joke with you. And I enjoy watching the two of you," Frank replied.

Benito was such a practical joker and terrible tease that no one wanted to be his *campero* so he always operated alone except for his dog – his only company. Benito had worked for the Patrón for over twenty years. He never changed. Always the same Benito! He knew his

sheep and they loved their *pastor*. He could call all the *negras* by name.
Other *pastores* did not like to replace Benito when he took leave, for his
sheep had a terrible habit of walking twice as far as regular sheep.
Because of the sparse grass in the areas of Russia where they were originally from, it seemed to be their inherent nature to be great wanderers.
Only Benito could keep up with them. The Patrón would often say jok-
ingly, "Benito is as lightfooted as they are – and looks like them."

Benito reported to his Patrón. But this day he saw a faraway look
in Don José's eyes. Benito did not comment, for he also noticed Don
José was not as talkative and felt certain things were not well with his
Patrón. After spending a short while with Benito, Frank and Don José
left and arrived at Galisteo in time to hear the *cencerro* ring for dinner.

Don José was spending a lot of time walking and doing what exercise
his body allowed him. One day, as he was sitting by himself on the long
bench in front of his store, he felt a presence. After quietly visiting with
this spirit, he determined it was his father, Don Juan. The time had come
to look back through his life. While he sat there, the events of his entire
life unfolded. He saw himself as a child asking his father to tell him the
story of how their ancestors had travelled from Spain to this country.
And about the Indian raids on the village. Then, he saw himself as a
young man with all his ambitions and dreams and finally, the hard work
and dedication that made all those dreams come true. He saw his loved
ones, especially Frank, who had worked by his side. "Will Frank continue
on with my work or will there be changes or a turn of events which will
end my fondest dreams?" he wondered. "Frank is wise, and if they let him
go on he will continue to hold the ranches together. Our people who
work for us trust him and they will be loyal to him as they have been to
me." He glanced across the street at Doña Josefa Davis' hacienda which
he had given to Frank and wondered what Frank would do with it.
"Maybe some day he will live in it and hear all the spirits of the past tell
him their stories." The old hacienda had seen most of the important
history of Galisteo being made. The people it had housed as guests included everyone from Archbishops to Governors and, of course,
Generals from both the Union and Confederate Armies.

Don José was feeling all this history that day as he also felt the presence of Don Juan. He was peaceful now for this was the first time he had really experienced Don Juan's closeness. As he was daydreaming he was awakened by the voices of some small children playing down the road. He arose from the bench and slowly walked around the corner of the street toward where he had heard their voices. As he approached the children, he noticed they were pelting a truck which belonged to a family of *gringos* who had recently moved into the village from back east. There were no *gringos* living in Galisteo up to this time. These people had found the village quiet and peaceful and had decided to buy a property from Don José. He asked the oldest child in the group throwing rocks, "Why are you doing this harm to a man's truck? You children know better than to do this!"

One of the most outspoken answered, "They don't belong here. And they are *gringos*. Before long, they will take over."

Don José called them over and told them, "No one will take over unless you allow them to. But stones and hurt to these people – or any other people – will not scare them away. You must learn to live with all people for the greatest threat you have is yourselves. Educate yourselves. Study hard. Read about the world. And most importantly, pray to your God!"

The children looked at him. Most of them did not understand. But that day the Patrón understood – he understood what the future would hold for many of his people. He would hope and pray that his people would learn to live with the *gringo*, not be subservient to him but live as equals with respect and dignity. Years later they would profit from cooperating with everyone and the country would grow even stronger. He walked away, quietly brushing a tear from his cheek.

Shortly after this, the Patrón became weak and he suffered a stroke which, together with the advancing Parkinson's condition, forced him to leave Galisteo and take to his bed in Santa Fe. With the loving care of his wife and daughters, he spent the last years of his life in relative comfort. His friends and family visited with him and tried to keep him busy. His greatest joy, of course, remained Frank and his visits. Frank would come at least twice a week and make a full report to his father, never letting on for one moment that the Patrón probably would never return again to Galisteo or to his beloved *Agua Verde*.

In December Nineteen hundred fifty-one, the Patrón passed away quietly at his Santa Fe home. His job as caretaker was over.

The news of Don José's death traveled fast. His many loyal workers and friends were shocked and saddened. What would happen now? Don José was a way of life to many of them. Of course there was Frank, but it was too early to speculate as to what changes would take place without the Patrón.

Don José was buried in Santa Fe, which was an unusual request of his, but one which was honored by his family. Many years before he had told Frank he did not want his dead body in the area he loved so much. He wanted only his living body to have ever been on the land that meant so much to him. The Funeral Mass and burial were attended by the many people who had been fortunate to know or to serve the Patrón. Truckloads of families from the *Agua Verde* came to spend his funeral day with him. It came as a surprise to hear the many heart-felt comments they expressed to the mourning family of Don José – surprising because so many of the close family members never realized the genuine love his people felt for him.

You would expect the story to end here, but it could not end when the last Patrón was gone. As death often does, it had to give life and hope to others. Modern times were upon this country and the changes that were taking place were taking place so quickly that most people could not understand why there had ever been a Patrón System in the first place. Values were now being replaced by quick and easy answers.

Don José's estate was distributed as he requested. He had named Frank to administrate his estate which Frank did for a short time. But, following discord within his family, Frank soon turned over the estate to his mother and two of his sisters. Frank devoted his time to his own holdings and livestock his father had left him. He was distressed and unhappy about the events that had transpired, but he had learned from Don José, who would say, "This is God's will!"

The people in the *Agua Verde* area and others who worked for the

Patrón scattered to the four winds. A few went to work for Frank on his ranches. Others held on until Doña Pablita and two of her daughters sold the *Agua Verde* to an oil millionaire from Roswell. They also sold the Galisteo properties to a wealthy building contractor from El Paso. All was gone! It happened so fast – what had taken so long to build and with so much work had been turned over to new caretakers. The last traces of Don José's work would be visible only with Frank's holdings, for Frank had been given the very best lands by his father. These lands also were some of the original lands that Don Juan had given Don José.

Frank suffered great hurt. It was difficult for him to see an end to the accumulation of so many years of work. But he truly was the son of Don José and he decided to begin anew. He would tell his beautiful and understanding wife, "Maria, we will not quit. We have land and my father and his father began with just the land." He felt this deeply and was resolved to continue with his father's work even if for the time it would have to be on a smaller scale. He understood the changes that were taking place. Some of the people who had once been content with the Patrón System were suddenly calling it a disgrace and a wretched way to have lived. Frank did not feel he could argue with them. He could understand the philosophies of the times. His only defense was founded in these people and their offspring: They were still here to criticize and complain compared to the many who had not survived the Depression and other hard times.

Frank began by restoring a part of the Sylvester and Josefa Davis hacienda which had been given to him by his father. Eventually it housed his store and cantina and from it he continued to operate his livestock business. His ranch headquarters he located a mile north of Galisteo at a vacated lambing station he named *Las Marias*. There were only a few buildings left there, but with the help of a handful of loyal workers soon *Las Marias* blossomed into a very workable ranch headquarters. He built an addition to the old existing house, making a fine home. He built a good set of corrals and a sturdy barn. His lands extended for over thirty miles – from the center of Galisteo to the ghost town of *Ojo de la Vaca* (Cowsprings). In time he would add more land until finally his holdings would traverse two counties. It would never be as large as that he and his father had held together, but for all purposes it would be his "miniature *Agua Verde.*"

Frank retained a number of the best *vaqueros* the Patrón had employed for many years. God was good to Frank: his herds of cattle increased and his other businesses prospered. Since he had always favored raising cattle, he sold the sheep. Frank and his family worked hard. His children were educated in the best schools. Twenty-two years after his father's death when Eternal Rest would call him to join the Patrón, Frank would leave fulfilled and content, for in his own way he had been true to his father's wishes – to be a good caretaker and to help his people.

With Frank's great respect for history and his wish for others to be able to experience and touch a bit of the past, he left the collection he had assembled and housed in his store to speak to us – now the Galisteo Historical Museum. Here are the pack saddles used by the *camperos*, the riding chaps of Reyes Montoya, the whip of Benito Vigil, as well as furniture, religious aritcles and personal effects belonging to the Patrón. These and letters and documents indeed bear witness to the past.

With all these things achieved in his life, Frank and his beautiful Maria left this earth almost together, five months apart.

Don José, the *Last Patrón*, and Frank, the *Patroncito* were reunited. They must have a new dream by now.

Frank and his beautiful María.

afterword

Medicinal herbs and their use by the Spanish-speaking people of New Mexico are mentioned throughout this book. Therefore, in order to provide you more knowledge about the herbs and their uses, the author would like to share with you the results of his work and to discuss his knowledge of them with you. The herbs were sure to be found in every household. The information is presented in the form of a story and tells of some of the people who used the herbs in the Galisteo and *Agua Verde* areas during the time of the Last Patrón...as well as today.

Ajo   *allium sativum*   **Garlic**

In Galisteo, garlic has had many uses. As a preventative against diphtheria it is worn around the neck by people who might have the disease. Used also as a remedy to relieve pain in the stomach; two garlic cloves are baked, then crushed, water added, then the mixture is drunk. For toothache, a clove is pressed against the gum.

Alamo de la   **Valley**
Hoja Redonda   *populus wislizeni*   **Cottonwood**

The old ladies of the tiny village have great faith in the bark, leaves and branches of the alamo. The bark was roasted and the ashes mixed with corn meal to make a cure for boils. The leaves of the tree were boiled and the results were taken to relieve dropsy. For bone fractures, the rough bark was cooked over a low fire, the liquid strained and cooked again until it was like honey. This was spread over the fracture for healing.

Alamo Sauco   *populus angustifolia*   **Mountain Cottonwood**

Doña Luisa, an old medica in Galisteo, advised dipping a wad of cotton into the ripe fruit and placing it on swollen gums or on a painful tooth. Doña Luisa also said that the fresh flowers used as a tea was the best remedy for purifying the blood.

Albaricoque   *prunus armeniaca*   **Apricot**
It was common practice that, when a child suffered from dryness of the nose, a poultice be made from the ground kernel of the pit and applied. This same preparation was applied to the throat of people who suffered from goiter.

Alfalfón   *melilotus alba*   **Sweet Clover**
The lovely ladies of Galisteo would, in the spring of the year, go into the fields and pick alfalfón for use in their linens and finer things as a sweet-scent and also to keep bedbugs away.

Alhucema   *lavandula*   **Lavender**
This beautiful and fragrant flower was brought from Spain into New Mexico and was carefully guarded during the winter. It was used for fumigating sickrooms. As a tea, it was used for colic and also to relieve vomiting and stomach troubles. Alhucema and manzanilla together, helped regulate menstrual flow. The two herbs are mixed and applied with a cloth.

Aloe Vera   *aloe socotrina*   **Aloe Vera**
A pinch of this succulent cactus, when used as a snuff, will clear your nasal passage. When a fresh piece is removed from the plant and applied on an open wound, it will usually stop the bleeding. The liquid from this plant when applied to the face will smooth the skin.

Altamisa   *artemisia franserioides*   **Aster Family**
The entire plant is used as a tea for people suffering from colic, bad colds and diarrhea. It was considered an excellent tea for general health.

Alvacar   *ocimum basilicum*   **Sweet Basil**
Don Juan Ortiz, a Patrón of Galisteo, always advised those who wanted money and good luck to carry some of the herb in their pockets. The people believed that the leaves mixed with oil and dropped into the ear was a sure cure for earaches. The herb is taken as a tea for weak stomach and for the appetite.

Amole   *yucca baccata-glauca*   **Yucca**

In this village, ground amole root was used by the people for washing purposes. They believed that the amole promoted hair-growth. The native people also used the amole as a remedy for gonorrhea. A wine syrup was also made which was considered beneficial for rheumatic joints.

Añil   *helianthus annus*   **Sunflower**

Of course the children of the village sought out the seed for their taste. The older people, however, cherished the sunflower in preparing a bath for rheumatism and arthritis. A poultice of the mashed plant was said to help relieve chest pains.

Añil del Muerto   *verbesina encelioides*   **Gold Weed**

This plant is smaller and has gray foliage to differentiate it from the regular sunflower. For stomach trouble, the leaves are ground and a tea is prepared. This tea is also used for rheumatism. It is also believed that a tea is good for liver problems. In the treatment of canker sores, the entire plant is ground. A little olive oil is applied to the sores and then sprinkled with the herb powder. A remedy for piles is a mixture of Añil del Muerto and tobacco which is then applied to the area.

Anís   *pimpinella anisum*   **Anise**

In the Galisteo Basin, anís was used as a tea to help remove liquids from people suffering from diabetes. The tea was also used for stomach trouble and coughs. An old fable suggested that a parrot would talk if you fed it anise seeds.

Azafrán   *carthamus tinctorius*   **Saffron**

For measles, this was a sure cure. The herb is soaked in cold water until the liquid is yellow. The fluid is then strained and drunk half a glass at a time to bring out the rash and reduce the fever. An ointment made of Azafrán and butter is used to draw infection from wounds. It is also used to invigorate the heart.

Baras de San José   *penstemon torreyi*   Hollyhock

The most popular flower growing in the gardens of the people in the area is the many-colored and aristocratic hollyhock. The flowers were used to make a tea which was believed to relieve chest colds and strengthen the kidneys. The tea was also used to act as a blood purifier and to remove varicose veins.

Bellota de Sabina   *phoradendron juniperinum*   Mistletoe

Besides providing a free kiss on occasion, it is also used to cure venereal diseases. A tea is prepared by boiling the berries and drunk until a cure takes place. Bellota tea is also excellent for stomach trouble and for purifying the blood.

Cadillos   *xanthium commune*   Cockleburr

The sheepeherders who roamed with the flocks in the basin sang perhaps the highest praise for the cadillo. Three little burrs were boiled in a cup of water and drunk as a sure cure for a bad case of diarrhea. A poultice made of the burrs and green leaves mixed with a little oil was good for healing cuts and wounds.

Calabaza   *cucurbitaceae*   **Pumpkin**

Pumpkin seeds are ground and a tea prepared from them to remove tapeworms from the body. The Spanish women and men felt that by eating pumpkin seeds their virility would be maintained.

Calabazilla   *cucurbita foetidissima*   **Wild Gourd**

As a visitor to Galisteo in the summertime, you will notice the abundance of wild gourds growing within the village walls. The roots of the plant are said to go six feet deep. The gourd can be fatal if eaten in quantity. The pulp and seeds make a fine shampoo to promote hair growth.

Caña Agria   *rumex hymenosepalus*   **Wild Pieplant**

One of the most popular roots to cure pyorrhea. It is used as a mouth rinse. Canaigra tea is used as a gargle for sore throats. The powdered root is applied under the arms or between the legs to alleviate skin irritations.

Canela   **Cinnamon**

The mothers could effect a fast cure of a stomach ache by preparing a hot tea of canela. Children would also like to chew on the cinnamon sticks as a substitute for candy.

Canutillo del Campo   *ephedra torreyana*   **Mormon Tea**

Captain Sylvester Davis, one of the first Anglos to arrive in Galisteo, had great faith in canutillo tea and drank large quantitles to alleviate rheumatic and arthritic pain. The people drank it also to cure venereal disease. Canutillo is also regarded as a wonderful cure for kidney trouble and as a diuretic.

Cardo Santo   *argemone hispida*   **Thistle Poppy**

The Spanish people mashed the roots, added a little olive oil and used it to relieve earaches. For toothaches, the roots were used as a tea and held in the mouth to relieve pain. Many people used the entire plant in preparing a bath to cure rheumatism, dropsy and swellings.

Cebolla   *allium cepa*   **Onion**

The Spanish men are great at eating onions raw or cooked for they believe that onions give them bodily and mental strength. During a severe case of chills, the people would roast onion slices and apply them all over the body.

Chamisa   *atriplex canescens*   **Saltbush**

Chamisa was used principally by the people to relieve stomach pains. The green leaves are chewed and washed down with a glass of water.

Chan *salvia reflexa* **Wild Sage**

Many people eat the dry or green leaves with a little salt to cure a severe case of colic. The men of the area, however, feel that the same tea, drunk as often as possible, increases their virility and returns their *machismo* to them.

Chaparro **Rabbit Bush**

Chaparro was a cure found strictly in the Galisteo area. The chaparro limbs were wrapped in a small cloth and immersed into the bath water as a cure for rheumatism.

Chicoria *taraxacum officinale* **Dandelion**

The old *curandero* would recommend a pinch of its flowers to be boiled until the water turned yellow; a glassful should be taken daily for a month as a cure for heart trouble. The raw or cooked greens savored with a little vinegar were said to purify the blood. The dry ground leaves made into a paste with water or oil are applied to a bad bruise to insure healing.

Chile *capsicum* **Chili**

Chile, the famous New Mexican product, was regarded as one of the great health foods. Red chile is known to cure rheumatism when prepared by splitting open a pepper, soaking it in vinegar, then applying the liquid to the painful areas. Chile is eaten in great quantities and is considered a remedy for heart trouble, asthma, constipation and as an aid for virility.

Chimajá *aulospermum purpureum* **Wild Parsley**

Above all other herbs, chimajá was a prize to have in the household. The dry leaves and flowers are boiled into a tea and taken for debility and stomach trouble. Every cantina in the area had a bottle of whiskey containing a sprig of the plant. This was called *mestela* which, when aged long enough, made a drink fit for kings.

Cilantro   *coriandrum sativum*   **Coriander**

Cilantro, perhaps, found great grace in the hands of the village house-wives – for they would mix the seeds in just about all their savory meat dishes. Cilantro is also used to stop a toothache and relieve stomach pain when used as a tea.

Comfré   *symphytum officinale*   **Comfrey**

Comfré was scarce in the area but the people had great faith in its power as a tea for curing ulcers, kidney trouble and lung trouble. Being rich as a skin moisturizer, the women swore that it would remove wrinkles and signs of aging.

Coronilla   *gaillardia pinnatifida*   **Blanket Flower**

In Galisteo coronilla is known as *hilotito* and is used for colds or headaches by crushing the stems, adding water and applying to the forehead. The people also take a pinch of crushed coronilla and use it as a snuff for fast relief of a head pain.

Cota   *thelesperma gracile*   **Wild Tea**

Cota is a famous general health tea which promotes relaxation and is thought to be of great value in its powers of virility. It is also considered a fine diuretic.

Culantrillo   *coriandrum sativum*   **Coriander**

Culantrillo is the plant of the cilantro. It was used to make a tea which was considered very good to relieve bloating. It was also considered a general health tea.

Dill   *anethum graveolens*   **Dill**

If you like to read and write a lot but tire easily, fix yourself a cup of dill tea and sip it while you work. It stimulates your thinking processes. Dill is wonderful as a tea to expel gas and quiet your nerves.

Dormilon *rudbeckia tagetes* **Coneflower**
This strange herb found its fame amongst the women of the area – for it was considered the best emenogogue for female troubles. A strong tea was made of its leaves, a little honey added and a cup drunk every morning. The same remedy was also thought to cure gonorrhea.

Durazno *prunus persica* **Peach**
Spanish Americans used the peach leaf as a tea for asthma and used peach bark boiled in water to reduce high fever. We must remember, however, that peach leaves contain some hydrocyanic acid, one of the five most dangerous poisons known. Caution must be taken in its use.

Entraña *opuntia arborescens* **Cactus**
This particular plant is the upright and must not be confused with the low-growing cholla. The people used the roots as a hair tonic to prevent falling hair and stimulate growth. The roots are soaked in water for two or three days before application.

Escoba de la Víbora *gutierrezia tenius* **Snake Weed**
The "broom of the snake" was used as a tea for cure of snakebites and for rheumatism. The herb also was considered excellent in the preparation of suppositories for the relief of female troubles. A cooked decoction of the plant was also used for douching in cases of infection.

Estafiate *artemisia mexicana* **Black Sage**
In the Galisteo Basin, where the estafiate grows profusely, it is considered highly beneficial to relieve stomach troubles or internal pain when taken as a tea. A bath is also prepared for rheumatism.

Flor de San Juan *anogra runcinata* **Evening Primrose**
The Flor de San Juan is boiled in water, a little sugar is added and it is then drunk to alleviate kidney trouble. As a poultice, it is said to help relieve sore throats.

Flor de Santa Rita   *castilleja integra*   **Indian Paintbrush**
Here is a rich and colorful flower that grows along the Galisteo River and the people considered it a fine diuretic. A tea was brewed of the plant and drunk as often as possible during the day to effect a cure.

Frijoles   *phaseolus vulgaris*   **Pinto Beans**
Although frijoles have always been considered important in the food of the native people, they also consider frijoles as medicinal. To remove dust or other particles from the eye, a bean is inserted. The green leaves of the frijoles, soaked in vinegar and water, are applied to the head to remove sunstroke. Women were given a bean tea to aid in eliminating after birth.

Garbancillo   *lupinus aduncus*   **Quaker Bonnets**
The villagers from Galisteo felt that bathing sores or facial eruptions with a tea made from the leaves was beneficial in healing them. This plant is considered poisonous if taken internally.

Geranio   *pelargonium*   **Geranium**
Besides the great beauty that they bring to the low-lying adobe homes in the Galisteo Basin, the glorious geranium can cure an earache when the leaves are warmed and placed on the ear. Also, the leaves can be mashed, a little vinegar and salt added, and placed on the forehead to relieve a headache.

Guaco   *cleome serrulata*   **Stinkweed**
As you drive through northern New Mexico in the fall of the year, a profuse purple coloration that dots the roadsides is the herb guaco. As a tea, it is considered a cure for anemia, for grippes in the intestines and crushed leaves placed on insect bites will stop the inflammation. Many Spanish people cook the tender leaves and eat them with chile.

Habas *vicia faba* **Horsebeans**
As a cure for chest colds, the habas are roasted in the oven and boiled,
salt is added and the soup drunk. A paste can be made from the same
mixture and applied to the chest and back to cure pneumonia. Pulverized
habas held in the mouth will cure mouth sores.

Hueso de Cerezo *prunus cerasus* **Cherry Stone**
Don José Ortiz, the old Patrón of Galisteo, swore that a tea made with
the boiled cherry pits strengthened his kidneys.

Inmortal *asclepiodora decumbens* **Antelope Horns**
The "herb of immortality," cherished by people who suffered from heart
tremors, was applied as a poultice over their hearts to obtain a cure. A
small amount of powdered root mixed with water will reduce any kind
of internal pain. It was administered in the same manner to aid labor
pain during childbirth.

Jarita *salix exigua* **Sandbar Willow**
The leaves and the branches are chewed to strengthen the gums and
teeth. Doña Josefa would say, "Chew jarita every day and keep your
teeth another day."

Lechones *asclepias latifolia* **Milk Weed**
The people felt that for severe cases of facial pain the milk drawn from
the herb was to be applied. The milk of the herb was also used for skin
discoloration and to remove freckles.

Lengua de Vaca *rumex crispus* **Rumex**
Because of its high quantity of tanin, this plant is considered poisonous;
however, the green leaves are mashed and applied to the forehead to
relieve a headache. A small amount of the root can be chewed and spat
out to cure pyorrhea.

Limoncillo   *pectis angustifolia*   **Aster Family**
The simple little plant with the lovely lemon-like odor was recommended by the village *curandero* to relieve stomach aches and stomach cramps.

Lirio   *iridaceae*   **Iris**
The tubers of the iris contain poison and should never be eaten. However, the native people tied lirio roots around the neck of a person suffering from smallpox. Smallpox was believed to close the throat and the lirio root was believed to keep it open.

Maíz   *zea mays*   **Corn**
Be it Indian or yellow corn – besides being a popular staple – it is soaked in water overnight and the liquid drunk to strengthen the prostate gland. The same tea with a little honey added can also be used to treat kidney disorders.

Malva del Campo   *malva parviflora*   **Mallow**
Doña Josefita Davis, whose home is now the Galisteo Historical Museum, believed that malvas could cure anything. A tea is prepared from its leaves to relieve fever, to cure pimples, headaches, for women's complaints and to expel afterbirth.

Manzanilla   *matricaria courrantiana*   **Camomile**
When Labriano Anaya suffered from an earache, the dry flowers were warmed and applied to his ear to effect a cure. Manzanilla tea was used as a general sedative and for female trouble, stomach aches, heart trouble, colds and as a hair rinse. Here is a herb that is all-powerful and is capable of many cures.

Maravilla   *quamoclidion multiflorium*   **Wild Four O'Clock**
High fever can be reduced by mixing the powdered leaves with olive oil and rubbing it over the entire body. Many people used the same application to cure goiter. For dropsy, the dry roots are mixed with tobacco and applied to the body. Maravilla tea supposedly controls overeating.

Marijuana   *cannabis sativa*   **Marijuana**

The modern world is using this herb for its depressant effects similar to liquor, but the native people considered it a cure for asthma and rheumatism when smoked.

Mariola   *artemisia rhizomata*   **Sage Brush**

The custom in Galisteo was to give a child a fresh or dry leaf to chew to cure a simple stomach ache. A tea made from mariola was believed to cure rheumatism and arthritis.

Mastranzo   *marrubium*   **Horehound**

Most Anglos are familiar with his herb. As a cure for coughs and sore throats, the leaves are boiled, a little honey is added, then the mixture is drunk as often as necessary. A hot foot bath of mastranzo leaves aids in curing rheumatism and frozen feet. A thick gravy made from mastranzo and starch is said to cure stomach pains and colic.

Moradilla   *verbena ambrosiaefolia*   **Verbena**

Of all the herbs in Galisteo Basin, this is the favorite of the author, José Ortiz y Pino, not only because of its purple beauty but also when used as a tea it has a great calming effect. If he has pain in his back, he makes a poultice and applies it.

Mostaza Amarilla   *brassica campestris*   **Mustard**

A bath is prepared with a cup of mustard seed to cure rheumatism. A beautiful mustard plaster is made by mixing flour, water and ground mostaza and applying it with a cloth to the painful area.

Nopal   *opuntia*   **Prickly Pear**

The spines must be removed from the fruit of the nopal cactus, then it is roasted and bound with a cloth on the body to cure swellings. When a woman is ready to bear child the fruit is mixed with eggs and cooked, then eaten by her to increase her milk flow.

Orégano de la Sierra   *monarda menthaefolia*   **Horsemint**
Orégano de la sierra differs from the orégano del campo in that it pro-
duces heavier clusters of lowers and the stems are thicker. The people
would search for this herb and use it as a tea to relieve daily tensions.

Orégano del Campo   *monarda*   **Horsemint**
It is not the chile alone but the orégano in it that makes the chile what it
is. For a cough, a tea is made and drunk as often as needed. It is also
great for stomach pains. Orégano is considered a general health herb
and has a variety of uses.

Oshá   *ligusticum porteri*   **Parsley Family**
When Doña María knew that her husband, Don Luis, would come
home in the evening feeling no pain from a night out, she would immediately prepare a piece of oshá root in a glass of whiskey and, upon
his rising in the morning, would make him drink it and life would be
beautiful for him. Oshá was also used to remove stomach gas and to
cure a cold and a chronic cough. The oshá root could be made into a tea
or chewed to effect these cures.

Pagué   *dysodia papposa*   **Fettid Marigold**
Pagué is another of the general health herbs which people used to cure
ills from coughs to stomach problems. The fresh leaves when chewed
are excellent in expelling gas.

Paja   **Straw**
The Finnish people have their sauna baths; the natives in this area boil a
bucket full of straw in water, add hot stones, wrap a blanket about
themselves and place the bucket between their legs to effect a cure for
rheumatism.

Papas   *solanum tuberosum*   **Potatoes**
Raw potatoes sliced thinly are bound on the head and serve to draw
fever and relieve pain.

Pegapega   *mentzelia multiflora*   **Laosa Family**
When the herb is well ground, it is applied to rheumatic joints. The
people would pulverize it and make it into a poultice. Pegapega was
also used as the first glue to mend fragile Santos.

Pinhué   *hymenosyx floribunda*   **Colorado Rubber Plant**
Pinhué is usually confused in appearance with snakeweed, but its
makeup is more rubbery. During World War I, the government ex-
perimented in producing rubber from it. The people would chew the
roots and the pulp as it was thought to clense the teeth and also to calm
a sour stomach.

Piñón   *pinus edulis*   **Pine Family**
The native people would boil a small quantity of pine needles in water,
add a little piloncillo and use it to cure syphilis. Everyone has heard of
the piñon nut which the people felt, if eaten in quantity, kept the person
replenished in body oils.

Poléo   *mentha*   **Pennyroyal**
If a woman had a miscarriage, she was furnished with poléo leaves to
eat. It was felt that they would cleanse her. Poléo was used as a tea to
reduce fever, cure headaches and colds and given to women to drink
after childbirth.

Prodigiosa
There are many ladies in this area who swear that a tea made from this
herb is beneficial in aiding severe cases of diabetes. It is also believed to
purify the blood and aid in removing excess body liquids.

Punchón   *verbasum thapsus*   **Mullein**
Punchón was the first tobacco smoked by the native New Mexican and
later the people believed that the smoke was good for asthma as well as
if the leaves were soaked in whiskey and drunk they were also good for
the same complaint.

Rama de Sabina   *juniperus monosperma*   **Juniper**
Juniper twigs were boiled in water and a tea prepared to cure inflammation of the stomach and to relieve grippes in the intestines. It was also known to relax the muscles of a woman undergoing childbirth.

Reumático   *malvaceae*   **Mallow Family**
This herb, many times confused with the "herb of the negress," as they practically look alike except for their height, was used exclusively in preparing a bath to aid in curing rheumatism and for severe sprains.

Romerillo   *artemisia filifolia*   **Silver Sage**
Romerillo is often referred to as "the herb that is good to cure all ills." As a tea, it is considered a cure for indigestion, excessive gas and a general pain remover. The herb could also be added to bath water to cure rheumatism.

Rosa de Castilla   *rosa*   **Rose of Castille**
Here is a rose that came to the Galisteo Basin from Spain. When the buds start to bloom, the women of the village will pick them and dry them in the sun. Used as a tea, they are given credit for reducing high fever and curing sore throats.

Ruda   *ruta graveolens*   **Rue Family**
In cases that are referred to in this modern age as nervous tension, ruda was employed by the people as a cigarette mixture and smoked to relieve this problem. A tea was also used to effect sedation. The leaves could also be cooked and applied to the ear to cure an earache.

Tolache   *datura meteloides*   **Jimson Weed**
This is a very poisonous herb if eaten or smoked, but the ground seeds mixed with lard and applied to boils or skin irritations effect a cure. The dried leaves, crushed, are applied to piles. A bath made from the entire plant will cure colds and diarrhea.

Tomate del Campo *physalis neomexicana* **Ground Cherry**
This herb has been referred to as the Japanese Lantern because of the fine papery cover that encloses it. The people would either apply the ground green or ripe fruit with salt on the throat to cure tonsil trouble. People also stewed the berries with sugar to make a delectable jam.

Tomatito Pelón *solanum elaeagnifolium* **Bull Nettle**
Throughout the countryside in the Galisteo area, a small tomato-like pod appears on a tomato-like bush. It is not considered edible, but the people would crush the green cherry, add a little salt to it and bind it on the throat for swollen tonsils. When the berry is dry, it is ground and blown into the throat to cure catarrh and a simple headache.

Trementina de Piñón *pinus edulis* **White Pine Pitch**
A little bit of fresh trementina mixed with tobacco and salt and applied on the head will cure a headache. Dried pitch can be ground and rubbed on painful rheumatic areas. Piñon pitch can also be chewed and placed on a wound to heal.

Uña del Gato *acacia greggii* **Black Locust**
When an old *vaquero* suffered a painful fall from his horse, he would look for "cat's claws," pulverize them and apply the substance to his painful areas.

Yerba Buena *mentha spicata* **Spearmint**
We do not know of a single house in Galisteo that does not have fresh spearmint growing in its garden. For an upset stomach, for childbirth complications and overall general health, the tea of yerba buena has no equal. Many people drink the tea to bring relief to nagging pains of neuralgia. If you are prone to horrible hangovers, yerba buena tea can make you a good friend.

Yerba de la Golondrina   *euphorbia serpyllifolia*   **Spurge**
The "herb of the swallow" has found wide use in the healing of skin disease and warts. The plants secrete a milky substance which can be applied to remove warts. The plant, dry or fresh, can be applied as a poultice or drunk as a tea to relieve skin irritations.

Yerba de la Mala Mujer   *brickellia reniformis*   **Aster Family**
In the spring, there is not a *borreguero* who has grazed flocks in the basin who didn't search for a sprig of the "herb of the scarlet woman." It has a beautiful smell and can cure a toothache when it is boiled and the liquid held in the mouth.

Yerba de la Negrita   *sphaeralcea fendleri*   **Mallow Family**
The "herb of the negress" serves to remove tumors when the fresh leaves are made into a tea. To heal mosquito and ant bites, the herb is crushed, oil is added and the mixture applied to the irritated areas. A mashed leaves and flowers mixture, when used as a shampoo, is said to promote hairgrowth.

Yerba de la Tusa   *lepachys tagetes*   **Coneflower**
This yerba is boiled and a bath prepared when a person is suffering from major skin disorders. The same treatment is believed to help cure rheumatic pain.

Yerba del Buey   *grindelia aphanactis*   **Gum Plant**
The little golden buttons, which so easily cling to your clothing as you walk through the fields in this area, are regarded as a powerful diuretic. The buds and flowers are boiled in water, a little honey added and the tea drunk. For a severe case of paralysis, hot baths with the crushed herb are said to effect a cure.

Yerba del Caballo   *senecio filifolius*   **Groundsel**
It is said that the fastest way to rid yourself of a sore throat is to gargle with the "weed of the horse." Many people crush the herb, make a poultice and apply it to arthritic limbs.

Yerba del Manso   *anemopsis californica*   **Lizard's Tail Family**
When people suffered from suspected heart trouble, a tea was prepared and drunk in hopes of purifying the blood and strengthening the weak heart. Many people have drunk this same tea to cure internal infections. The crushed root is said to heal advanced pyorrhea.

Yerba del Pujo
What Ex-lax is to John Smith, yerba del pujo is to Herberto. The plant is boiled, strained and drunk until the necessary cure is reached.

Yerba del Sapo   *franseria tenuifolia*   **Aster Family**
The "herb of the frog" has long been considered a wonderful healer of open sores or open wounds when applied as a poultice. Many natives believe that a tea of the plant when drunk will help cure ulcers.

Yerba de San Pedro
This herb is local to Galisteo but cannot be found in large quantities. The people treated aches and pains by preparing a bath with the dry leaves and stems of the plant. The patient was put to bed and a cure effected when he began to sweat.

Zacate de Límon
During trips across Texas, the merchants would gather lemon grass and, upon their return, would plant it in their homes. A tea made from this grass is excellent for curing indigestion and other stomach disorders.

Zarzaparilla   *humulus lupulus*   **Wild Hops**
As a calmative and sedative, if you don't mind a little hypnotic effect, a tea from this herb will do the job. It is considered excellent for the blood, and as a general health tea. The roots are used in preparing a bath to cure dropsy.

For often I have heard the hardrocks I handled groan,
Because lichen and time and water dissolve them,
And they have to travel down the strange falling scale
Of soil and plants as the flesh of beasts to become bodies
          of men;
They murmur at their fate in the hallows of windless nights,
They'd rather be anything than human flesh played on by
          pain and joy.

"Margrave" —Robinson Jeffers

To look at any thing,
If you would know that thing,
You must look at it long:
To look at this green and say
"I have seen Spring in these
Woods," will not do — you must
Be the thing you see:
You must be the dark snakes of
Stems and Ferny Plumes of Leaves.
You must enter in
To the small silence between
The leaves,
You must take your time
And touch the very peace
They issue from.

John Moffitt

about the author

José Ortiz y Pino III, the grandson and namesake of *Don José, The Last Patrón*, is a graduate of New Mexico Military Institute and New Mexico State University. He has served as an officer in the U.S. Army, as a Santa Fe County Commissioner and as a New Mexico State Senator. He also served as Special Assistant to Governor David Cargo. As Chairman of the New Mexico State Parks Commission, he was instrumental in building the Villanueva State Park in San Miguel County and the Zoological and Botanical State Park at Carlsbad, New Mexico. Mr. Ortiz y Pino presently owns and operates the Galisteo Historical Museum. He is the author of numerous articles, short stories and books and is well-known for his knowledge of New Mexico plant life and its uses.